Coping with
ABORTION

Dr Judy Bury, the General Editor of this series, has worked in general practice and family planning for many years. She writes regularly on medical topics, and has a particular interest in self-help approaches to health care.

Other titles in the series include:
Coping with Caesarean and Other Difficult Births
Coping with Aging Parents
Coping with a Dying Relative
Coping with Sexual Relationships
Coping with Skin and Hair Problems
Coping with Periods
Coping with Your Handicapped Child
Coping with Rheumatoid Arthritis
Coping with Separation and Divorce

Coping with ABORTION

ALISON FRATER
BSc, MPhil

CATHERINE WRIGHT
BA, CQSW

With a Foreword by
ANNA RAEBURN

Chambers

© Alison Frater and Catherine Wright, 1986

Published by W & R Chambers Ltd Edinburgh

All rights reserved. No part of this publication may be reproduced, stored in a retrieval system, or transmitted, in any form or by any means, electronic, mechanical, photocopying, recording or otherwise, without the prior permission of W & R Chambers Ltd.

The illustrations are by Lyn May, courtesy of the Abortion Law Reform Association (copyright).

ISBN 0 550 20511 X

British Library Cataloguing in Publication Data

Frater, Alison
    Coping with abortion.
    1. Abortion
    I. Title II. Wright, Catherine
    363.4'6   HQ767
    ISBN 0-550-20511-X

Printed by Clark Constable, Edinburgh and London

Contents

1. INTRODUCTION 1
2. ARE YOU SURE YOU'RE PREGNANT? 9
3. DO YOU WANT AN ABORTION? 17
4. CAN YOU HAVE AN ABORTION? 38
5. WHAT DOES ABORTION INVOLVE? 50
6. HOW WILL YOU FEEL AFTER AN ABORTION? 63
7. SOME FINAL WORDS 78
  USEFUL ADDRESSES 80
  FURTHER READING 85

Alison Frater trained as a research biologist and now works for Brook Advisory Centres as Press and Information Officer. She has been involved in the pro-choice abortion movement both in Britain and abroad.

Catherine Wright is the Senior Social Worker at the Edinburgh Brook Advisory Centre. She has wide experience of counselling women with problem pregnancies.

Foreword

Abortion is something that most of us don't want to have to think about until it involves us or somebody we're close to. And there are circumstances which may arise where abortion becomes an alternative to be considered, even if in the past our faces have been totally set against it.

The argument is no longer about whether it should happen or not. Legally or illegally, it has happened for a very long time and it will go on happening, in every walk of life and every kind of society. Accordingly it becomes very important to see it in some sort of realistic context, to understand how the present Abortion Act came into being and what its provisions are. It is useful too to know what is involved in various therapeutic procedures, how you obtain them, what to do if you are obstructed and where to turn for help. Most importantly, this book considers how people feel about abortion and how they deal with those emotions, both before and after the abortion itself. Counselling, to help you face and understand your feelings or guide you towards contraception (if lack of it was part of the previous problem), is part of the experience of abortion.

The authors say 'Abortion is a choice you may not want to make, but it is your choice nevertheless.' This book does not make the choice for you. It seeks to inform you, calmly and kindly, so that you can make the choice for yourself.

Anna Raeburn
London, 1986

1. Introduction

> 'No society has controlled its fertility, or will do so before the end of the century, without recourse to a significant number of abortions.... It is perhaps the second oldest method of contraception (after coitus interruptus). It is known in every society. It is known in the villages of Pakistan. It is common in the shanty towns of Latin America but it always happens and it is not going to stop happening.'
>
> (Malcolm Potts, *The Guardian* 25.4.79)

Women with unwanted pregnancies have always resorted to abortion. Throughout history, and still in many countries with restrictive abortion laws, women subject themselves to the danger and misery of an illegal abortion in far from ideal conditions. Others face the dilemma of travelling miles from home to a foreign country where abortion is legal. In 1984 almost 33 000 abortions carried out in Britain on non-residents included over 20 000 women from Spain and nearly 4000 from the Irish Republic.

Is this book for you?

If you're pregnant and unsure about what to do, this book is intended to help you find an unbiased source of information and support. If you decide to seek an abortion, it will help you find your way through the system quickly and safely. If you have already had an abortion, you may find that reading the book makes sense in retrospect of what may have been a confusing and distressing time.

Abortion is a common and safe procedure. But it does stir up a lot of emotions and can appear very complicated. This chapter provides a background, placing abortion in a social and historical context. Before you do anything else you need to be sure that you are pregnant: Chapter 2 discusses the symptoms of pregnancy and where you can go for pregnancy tests. Chapter 3 examines the conflicting emotions you may have about your pregnancy, suggests practical ways of understanding them and is a guide to reaching the decision that's going to be best for you. Chapter 4 details the options you have when seeking an abortion, where to go for help and why some places will be better for you than others: it also offers an explanation of why women often encounter difficulties when seeking abortion. Methods of abortion before and after 12 weeks are discussed in Chapter 5 together with their relative safety and how to take care of yourself afterwards. Chapter 6 looks at the complex of emotions you are likely to feel after an abortion.

Coping with Abortion was written to set down the facts that women need when seeking abortion and to suggest ways of coping before, during, and after. Abortion is a choice you may not want to have to make, but it is your choice nonetheless.

Legalised abortion provides women who wish to control their fertility with access to safe methods of terminating an unwanted pregnancy. And where information about contraception is tied in with abortion services, future unwanted pregnancies are more likely to be averted than they are for women who have to resort to a criminal abortionist. Safe, legal abortion has been available in Britain for some years but this hasn't always been the case.

History of abortion law in England and Wales

There were no laws on abortion until the 19th century. The first restrictive Act of Parliament on abortion was introduced in 1803, although few prosecutions resulted and abortionists still openly advertised their illicit services.

'Ladies — lost happiness regained — any lady of respectability involved in distress from any expectation of inevitable dishonour may obtain consolation and security and a real friend in the hour of anxiety and peril by addressing a line to ....'

> Bells Court and Fashionable Magazine
> September 1807.

The 1861 Offences Against The Person Act — a more formidable statute — made abortion illegal and recommended strict prison sentences, even death, for abortionists. The wording of the act that abortion was 'illegal when procured unlawfully' suggested that there were circumstances where abortion could be legal. This loophole was not exploited until the Bourne judgement in 1938. Until then abortion was considered legal only when necessary to save the woman's life.

Undeterred by the law, barbers, hairdressers, tobacconists and herbalists continued to profit from abortifacients (substances said to cause an abortion) and criminal abortion was rife. Advertised as 'A boon to womankind' or 'cures for female ills of every kind', these so-called remedies included colocynth (bitter apples), hiera-picra (hikey-pikey), tansy, pennyroyal, apiol combined with steel, gin and salts, iron and aloes, caraway seeds, turpentine, washing soda and quinine. Abortion was often a side effect to the muscular spasms and contractions caused by such noxious substances. Lillie Langtry revealed that this practice continued in the late 19th century, in letters to her lover Edward VII, then Prince of Wales.

> 'My own darling, I am not sure yet ... I am sure there must be something wrong or what I took would have made me ... Please go to the chemist and ask how many doses one ought to take a day as I must go on taking it ...'

Abortionists were not all exploitative. Many acted out of compassion and sympathy. Those convicted were often women — mothers who, having suffered an unwanted pregnancy themselves, were trying to help out a friend or relative. Prosecutions of men were frequently of lovers or husbands caught helping their partner procure an abortion. Even those who did make a living from abortion often received tremendous loyalty from clients. It may have been a sense of guilt, complicity, or fear of blackmail, but women often protected practitioners from the police.

Wealthy women could still pay for the relative safety and discretion of a private abortion with a medical practitioner. But most women, denied access to doctors, bought their abortions in the back street, risking both their health and their liberty.

Complications leading to septic abortions were common and there were between 50 and 60 deaths due to abortion every year. In 1933, the Birkett Committee appointed by the government to research the abortion problem, estimated that there were at least 60 000 criminal abortions a year. Reputable gynaecologists of the time put the figure much higher, at around 250 000. The committee recommended liberalising the abortion law to include circumstances where pregnancy would be likely to endanger health as well as threaten the woman's life:

'Where continuance of pregnancy is likely to endanger her life or seriously impair her health.'

Although the outbreak of war prevented legislation to bring about these suggested reforms, the Bourne case in 1938 succeeded in widening the scope of the 1861 Act. The courts were asked to consider whether a doctor had acted unlawfully by terminating the pregnancy of a 14-year-old who had conceived after being brutally raped by two soldiers. The doctor, Aleck Bourne, told the police that he intended to perform an abortion and invited them to prosecute. When they decided to arrest him, the abortion had been done and he was charged with committing a criminal offence. Judge Macnaughten's decision in this case determined the law on abortion in England until the Abortion Act of 1967. He concluded that abortion could be lawful to prevent a woman becoming a 'mental and physical wreck' as well as to save her life. Nevertheless, women who managed to have abortions as a result of the Bourne decision were mostly those who could afford to pay a private fee.

After the Second World War, Britain was becoming a more literate, urban, industrialised society. Improved communication and better education meant that birth control methods, more easily publicised, became increasingly popular.

Introduction

High unemployment and low wages made many women keen to prevent unplanned pregnancies. The methods available included sheaths, rubber diaphragms and pessaries. They relied on the man's co-operation, were relatively inefficient, and an unaffordable expense for thousands of families living below the poverty line.

Women still turned to abortion, many with fatal results. But now public opinion, radicalised by war and scandalised by death due to abortion, pressed for reform of abortion laws.

The thalidomide tragedy of the early sixties further increased public awareness and parliamentary effort. A *Daily Mail* opinion poll in 1962 showed that 73% of the public was in favour of abortion where a child might be deformed. A Trog cartoon in *Private Eye* summed up the brutality of the government position on abortion. An overweight, self-satisfied doctor explains to a pregnant woman:

> 'I'm sorry but the ethical position is quite clear. Thalidomide was a legal prescription, but what you suggest is an illegal operation.'

During the sixties abortion became a major concern for women struggling for recognition and self-determination from a male-dominated parliament. Women, rebelling against the inevitability of the life of pregnancy and childbearing that their mothers had accepted, were using contraception (including the newly available contraceptive pill) to choose the number and timing of births. Many recognised that abortion is a necessary adjunct to contraception. More efficient use of contraception reduces the need for abortion but the latter will still be sought where methods fail or are overlooked.

Despite sustained and vehement opposition, mainly from Catholic MPs, pro-choice lobbyists managed to secure the passage of a liberal abortion Act in 1967. Opponents had achieved amendments to the original bill but the overall result was a major reform of abortion law. It had now been established that there may be social grounds for abortion and that abortion was legal if it was considered safer for the woman than the continuation of her pregnancy.

Abortion law in Scotland

The 1861 Offences Against the Person Act did not apply in Scotland. Abortions could be carried out by doctors for 'reputable medical reasons'. The legal boundaries were vague and not defined, but prosecutions were rare. Nevertheless, few doctors were willing to perform abortions. The Bourne judgement did not apply in Scotland and some say it would not have had the impact it did had it been brought in Scotland, because the courts would have failed to prosecute. The 1967 Act did not become part of Scottish law but, as in England and Wales, abortion in Scotland has become a common and safe procedure.

Abortion law in Ireland

The 1861 Offences Against the Person Act still applies in Northern Ireland but the 1967 Act does not, so abortion remains illegal except to save the woman's life. A woman in N. Ireland has the choice of travelling to Britain, enduring an unwanted pregnancy or subjecting herself to a backstreet abortion. There are active campaigns to extend the 1967 Abortion Act to N. Ireland. Abortion is illegal in the Republic of Ireland.

Abortion since 1967

Since the introduction of the 1967 Act fewer and fewer women have died following abortion. The Ministry of Health's Report on confidential enquiries into Maternal Deaths 1964/66 pointed out that of 133 deaths due to abortion, 98 were classified as due to 'illegal interference'. Death from illegal abortion is now almost completely unknown. There have been no such deaths since 1978. Abortion is now one of the commonest and safest operations performed in Britain. But still only half the women seeking abortion are helped by the National Health Service. The rest have to pay a private fee, usually with one of the abortion charities. There is considerable regional variation in abortion provision. A women living in the Northern Regional Health Authority is over four times more likely to be able to get an NHS

Introduction

abortion than a woman living in the West Midlands. Most of the women seeking abortions in Britain are single and over half are under 25.

The abortion rate in Britain for women of all ages rose dramatically after the introduction of the 1967 Act but from the early 1970s, as contraception has become more freely available, it has remained at around 1% of women a year.

There are strong reasons for maintaining good standards of abortion provision. No birth control methods are perfect and, for medical or even religious reasons, some women can't use the safest methods. Information on contraception is still not as well publicised or accessible as it should be and there is evidence that a substantial proportion of people don't use contraception in their early sexual encounters. Scares linking contraception with cancer or infertility often frighten people (unnecessarily) into deserting their reliable method for a less safe one or none at all. Where contraception fails, people are often likely to choose abortion since they were clearly not planning or expecting to conceive. Improved screening for foetal abnormality will also increase the need for safe abortion. Contraception and abortion have contributed to a reduction in unwanted babies for women of all ages. Among teenagers, while the birth rate has declined since the early 1970s, the abortion rate has been increasing very slowly with only about an 8% change in the last decade. For older women over 40 the conception rate, which fell between the late 60s and mid 70s, has been steady ever since, with roughly half choosing abortion rather than continuation of the pregnancy.

Strong emotions still surround the abortion issue. Since 1967 there have been no less than ten attempts to restrict abortion provision. Anti-abortionists argue that abortion is unethical and unjustified. Some say it is tantamount to murder and shouldn't be allowed in any circumstances. Others would agree to it only when the mother's life is in danger. Because of their vehement opposition to abortion many individuals and organisations have publicised stories and promulgated rumours to discredit the Abortion Act. Scandalous tales exaggerate the risks of abortion and are intended to horrify anyone who is contemplating terminating a pregnancy. It is difficult enough

Abortion

having to face an abortion decision, but to be exposed to such emotive propaganda can be a major source of hurt and guilt. Tremendous confusion is an inevitable result of unfounded rumours and can lead some people to the false conclusion that abortion is not available to them.

Some organisations who are opposed to abortion run refuges for single, pregnant women. While these may be fine for women wishing to continue their pregnancy, they often offer only temporary accommodation and tend to encourage adoption. Misleadingly, their advertisements closely resemble those of other organisations who support women with an unplanned pregnancy, including providing information about abortion. Women should beware of organisations offering prejudiced information.

The authors of this book are not pro-abortion but are pro-choice, believing that women should be allowed to decide for themselves what outcome they want for an unwanted pregnancy. We feel it's neither better nor preferable for any woman to have an abortion, but this should always be available as an option.

2. Are You Sure You're Pregnant?

'As soon as I woke up in the morning I knew I was pregnant.'

'I know it sounds strange, but I never really thought it would happen to me.'

'I felt quite special being pregnant, even though I knew I couldn't go through with it.'

It's very easy to get pregnant, especially if you have unprotected sex. Contraceptive methods vary in their efficiency, but none are 100% safe against pregnancy. There's always a possibility that your method will fail you. Don't forget there are methods of birth control that you can use after sex:

Abortion

The *morning-after pill* will protect against pregnancy if taken up to 72 hours after unprotected intercourse.

An *intra-uterine device* (also called coil, loop, or IUD) can be fitted in the womb for up to five days after unprotected sex. It works by preventing a fertilised egg implanting in the uterus. If medically suitable, the IUD could then stay in place and become your regular method of contraception.

How do you know if you are pregnant?

None of the symptoms of early pregnancy discussed below is absolutely reliable or definitely indicates pregnancy. Think about them rationally. What else is going on in your life that could produce these signs?

- Missing a period or having an unusually light period is often the first symptom to alert people to the possibility of a pregnancy. But there are other reasons for missing a period and worrying about a pregnancy is one of them.
- Nausea — so-called morning sickness — is an unpleasant symptom of pregnancy which may last for three months, sometimes less, sometimes longer. Most women don't just experience it in the morning. You may feel sick all day and particularly before meal times. Eating light biscuits can help, and sipping soft drinks or warm tea. But don't forget — not all pregnant women feel nauseated, especially early in pregnancy.
- Sore, swollen or heavy breasts. Even in early pregnancy the breasts may begin to swell as the milk glands mature.
- Needing to pee more often. This sometimes happens within a few days of a missed period.
- Feeling overweight or bloated. Water retention caused by pregnancy can often make you feel unusually heavy or uncomfortable.
- Going off certain foods or drinks, such as cheese, beer, coffee. The hormones released after conception can have a powerful effect on diet.
- Developing passions for foods is also common in pregnancy although this seems more usual at a later stage.

- Feeling unusually tired is a very common symptom in early pregnancy but there are of course many other causes of tiredness.

None of these symptoms means you are pregnant for sure. You can be pregnant and have none of them apart from a late or light period. Many women become pregnant at the beginning of a new relationship or when they're having an anxious or stressful time. But excitement, anxiety or stress can cause the symptoms of pregnancy. A change in lifestyle, concern over work, relationships, a new job, can make you miss a period, to say nothing of medical causes or being on the pill. Nausea, feeling bloated or wanting to pee are also signs of anxiety, and can also be due to something you've eaten, inadequate diet, or staying up late and drinking too much.

You may not be pregnant, but don't waste time trying to explain away the symptoms. Have a pregnancy test to find out for sure. Don't wait until you've missed two periods; most tests can be done 14 days after a missed period or sooner than that if you don't mind paying. Whether you're happy to be pregnant or not, the earlier you find out for sure the more time you will have to consider the options and get the appropriate care.

Pregnancy tests

Most pregnancy tests rely on a sample of urine, taken in the early morning when the hormones of early pregnancy are concentrated and so most easily detected. If you are more than 16 weeks pregnant, a urine pregnancy test may not work. At this stage, it's important to see a doctor for a physical examination to diagnose pregnancy. Some of the very early pregnancy tests use a blood sample. These tests are available from some abortion charities or in special circumstances from NHS facilities.

Collecting the urine sample

Collect the early morning urine sample in a clean bottle, jar or pot. Small jam jars are a good idea and old pill bottles will do. It's best to use something with an airtight lid. Remember that substances such as soap, detergent or bleach can affect a pregnancy test result, so rinse bottles etc. well when cleaning them out. You could always drop in to the clinic or surgery to

Abortion

which you're going to take the sample and collect a specimen bottle.

Hold the open bottle in the flow of first morning urine. You don't need to collect very much; only a few drops are needed for the test. About an eggcupful will certainly do.

The tester will ask for information on the date of your last period. You will also need to know the names of any drugs you're taking and your method of birth control, as these can affect the test result. Take the packet or bottles with you if you can't remember the name of your medication or contraception.

Timing of tests

Many women don't mind waiting 14 days after a missed period, which is the usual time to have a pregnancy test. Those who wish to have an earlier urine test can pay between £3 and £8 at one of the abortion charities or for a home kit, available from chemists. Early blood tests are available at one of the abortion charities or from commercial organisations. Some NHS facilities can offer early pregnancy tests on blood or urine in special circumstances.

In most NHS facilities such as doctors' surgeries, family planning clinics, or youth advisory centres your period has to be at least 2 weeks overdue before you can have a pregnancy test. Because of the disproportionate cost of the very early tests NHS places don't stock them or, if they do, will only help women who need the result urgently. They may be about to go on holiday or they may wish to have the injectable long-acting contraceptive or rubella immunisation and need to know if they're already pregnant. Where facilities do stock early tests they're often not advertised; so it may be worth phoning to ask. Organisations like the charity Pregnancy Advisory Service (PAS) or Marie Stopes in London can offer earlier tests by charging a fee proportionate to their cost. Some Brook Centres stock the early tests and some have to charge for any pregnancy test. Again it's worth phoning to ask for details of the service offered (see page 14).

Where to go for a pregnancy test

Where you go for a test may depend on what you want to do about your pregnancy. Chapters 3 and 4 present the options open to you and discuss why, if you want to choose abortion, you

Are You Sure You're Pregnant?

might decide to go to one place rather than another. All pregnancy testing facilities treat clients with complete confidentiality.

Family doctor. Your doctor may feel unable to refer you for abortion but would be very unlikely to refuse to do a pregnancy test.

Some family doctors don't have a pregnancy testing service. Others do efficient, on-the-spot pregnancy diagnosis. But in general most will send your early-morning urine sample away to a hospital laboratory for analysis. It may take between a few days and a week before you get the result. No GP should charge for pregnancy testing.

If you feel unsure about what to do if you are pregnant or have definitely decided on abortion you might not want to use such a slow service. You may prefer to use the time making your decision rather than waiting for a test result on which to base the decision.

A few doctors give hormone pills 'to bring on' a period. These are useless as you may bleed even if you are pregnant — and they delay your finding out for sure if you are.

Family planning clinics. Although most family planning clinics should offer pregnancy testing, some restrict their service to women who are already registered with them as contraceptive clients. You will be asked to bring a sample of early-morning urine from 14 days after a missed period. The address of your local family planning clinic will be in the telephone directory or available from directory enquiries. Your doctor's surgery or local Citizens Advice Bureau will certainly have the address or you can call the Family Planning Association clinic enquiry service 01-636 7866 for the address and telephone number of the family planning clinic most convenient to you.

Brook Centres. All except Coventry Brook offer pregnancy testing. Most tests are done 14 days after a missed period though earlier tests are available in some Brook Centres in certain cases. There are 19 Brook Centres in six cities in England and Scotland: Birmingham, Bristol, Coventry,

Abortion

Edinburgh, Liverpool and London. You will find them listed in telephone directories, or phone the central office at 153a East Street, London, SE17 2SD on 01-708 1234. Details of other youth advisory centres which offer pregnancy testing will normally be available from your local Citizens Advice Bureau.

Abortion charities. The abortion charities were set up to help women who were faced with the problem of an unwanted pregnancy (see page 45).

Pregnancy Advisory Service (PAS)
Head Office 11-13 Charlotte Street, London W1P 1HD. Tel: 01-637 8962. Branch at: The Cottage, 17 Rosslyn Road, East Twickenham, Middlesex (Tuesday and Thursday only). Tel: 01-891 6833.

This abortion charity based in London offers two pregnancy tests:

a urine test if your period is already at least 6 days late. It costs about £4. You will be given the result immediately.

a blood test which can give a result 14 days from the time you may have conceived and *before* a missed period. This costs about £8. Phone the next day for the result.

PAS have a 'walk in service'; no appointment necessary.

Marie Stopes House
The Well Woman Centre, 108 Whitfield Street, London, W1P 6BE. Tel: 01-388 0662.

Marie Stopes House is also based only in London and offers two pregnancy tests:

the standard early-morning urine test available with on-the-spot diagnosis from 14 days after a missed period costs about £5.

an early test done on a urine sample from 14 days after possible conception before a missed period costs about £8. For this, urine samples should be taken in before 11 a.m., for a result the same day (phone in the afternoons around 3 p.m.).

British Pregnancy Advisory Service (BPAS)
BPAS has branches in over 20 locations throughout Britain. Contact their head office at Austy Manor, Wootton Wawen, Solihull, West Midlands B95 6BX. Tel: Henley in Arden

Are You Sure You're Pregnant?

(05642) 3225 for details, or ask at your health centre or Citizens Advice Bureau. Their pregnancy test is available 6 days after a missed period and costs about £3. It's best to make an appointment although you're welcome to walk in to one of the centres if you don't mind waiting a while or being asked to return later if they're overbooked. You will be given the result within about 15 minutes.

Women's centres. Many women's centres have a pregnancy testing service. Some charge a small fee to cover their costs. Your local Citizens Advice Bureau should have details of their addresses and opening hours. You'll find they're probably only open for pregnancy testing a few hours a day. Most do the standard urine test 14 days after a missed period.

Chemists. Some chemists have an on-the-spot pregnancy testing service (large stores such as Boots do not). They always charge. Most are done on urine samples 14 days after a missed period.

Other commercial services. Organisations which do pregnancy tests for a profit can usually be found in most big cities. They are listed in telephone directories under 'Pregnancy testing' and have names similar to those of the charities.

Home kits or Do-It-Yourself pregnancy-testing kits. More and more women are using home kits bought from the chemist. Probably this is because they're becoming cheaper, more reliable, and some can be done 1 or 2 days after a missed period. These tests often have to be left for a couple of hours before the result (usually shown by a colour change) appears; so make sure you put it in an undisturbed place where it won't be knocked.

If you decide to use a home test but then go to your doctor, a Brook centre or a family planning clinic for advice, you will probably be asked to have another pregnancy test. Home kits are sometimes unreliable and the doctor or clinic may be suspicious of the result. You may well decide it's not worth the expense of an early test if you have to wait for 2 weeks anyway for a repeat test when you go for advice.

Tests by mail. Some women prefer the anonymity of sending a urine sample off through the mail to a private laboratory for analysis. Such services are advertised in magazines and newspapers or listed in the telephone directory. Because they do pregnancy testing for a profit, costs may be quite high. Make sure you use an airtight lid and a plastic bottle. Pack the sample carefully and don't forget to include your name and address. The laboratory will send the result within a few days, or you can phone them.

The result

If the result is positive it is very unlikely to be wrong. False positives do happen but are rare. When you go to see a doctor after a positive result, he or she will usually be able to confirm or dispute the pregnancy with considerable accuracy. If the result is negative but symptoms of pregnancy persist, then the test result may well be wrong. You should have another test within a few days. In the meantime don't forget to keep using contraception. If you miss another period and still have a negative pregnancy test, you should certainly consult a doctor.

An internal examination — what it is

If you are already over 8 weeks pregnant, a doctor can usually tell by examining you. After 16 weeks of pregnancy, examination is the most efficient way of diagnosis.

The cervix and uterus become softer and begin to enlarge during early pregnancy. To look for these changes the doctor will ask you to lie on the couch and remove lower garments including pants and tights. He or she will then gently enter your vagina with two fingers of one hand while pressing lightly on your abdomen with the other. The doctor usually wears surgical gloves using cream to lubricate the fingers so as not to hurt you. The examination may feel a little uncomfortable but shouldn't take longer than a few minutes. You will be expected to have an internal examination to confirm the result of a positive pregnancy test and if you are relaxed the discomfort is less. You can relax consciously if you tighten your muscles as if you were trying to stop yourself peeing, and then let go. An internal examination after a negative pregnancy test may discover a cyst or swelling inside the vagina which could have been causing the pregnancy symptoms.

3. Do You Want an Abortion?

The political debate surrounding abortion tends to disguise the fact that abortion is something which has to be dealt with on a personal level. Even if you have a clear political commitment to the idea that women should be able to have an abortion if they need one, you may be surprised at the strength of your emotions about pregnancy and abortion.

Whatever your situation and your previous opinions, your own pregnancy forces you to face fundamental questions about your life and what you want from it, what it means to have a child, and what you think parenting should involve. Even if you already have children another pregnancy will bring out these questions in another form.

If you are considering abortion you will have to go over what abortion means to you. Honest and careful appreciation of your reactions and the realities of your life will lead to a decision you can look back on with respect, whereas denial of these feelings is likely to lead to difficulties later on, especially if you did not look carefully at all the options.

This chapter is concerned with these emotional and practical issues. You may feel that you have already made a firm decision to seek abortion, or you may be reading this after you have carried out your decision, whichever way it went. Some of the things that may help you to make a decision are described in the following pages. You may find that some parts do not apply to you, but hopefully you will also find comments and descriptions which fit you and will be helpful. Later chapters cover what is involved in having an abortion and where you should go for help. You may feel so certain of your decision that you would rather turn straight to these chapters. Or you may feel that you need this practical information before you can consider what is being discussed in this chapter.

Abortion

Words

Words used in discussing an issue as sensitive as abortion are important. One of the hardest is what to call the foetus. Some of you will be in no doubt that 'it' is the only possible description, something alien that does not belong, but others will feel that 'it' is too impersonal.

At the early stages of pregnancy the foetus is not yet a baby, and to describe it as such can be very upsetting, as it conjures up images of a sweet cuddly baby in the centre of a loving family. This may be far from your reality if your pregnancy is a problem for you. 'Child' seems the best compromise; it is a little more distant, but is what you will be bringing up, if you decide to continue your pregnancy.

What kind of decision?

The decision to have a pregnancy terminated is unusual in that once done it is not reversible, it has to be taken in a limited period of time, and it is the responsibility of the woman alone which she may or may not choose to share with her partner. (The doctor has the right to refuse to do the abortion but the *woman* must request it in the first place). It is a serious decision, which can have important implications for your future. There will nearly always be some doubt, more for some people than for others, so you must be able to look back at your decision with the feeling that it was the best in the circumstances. In order to make this decision there are three important things that you should try to do:

1) *Try not to take the decision alone, and if possible speak to someone other than your partner.*
2) *Look carefully at the options available to you.*
3) *Listen honestly to your feelings and try to understand them.*

When you first find out you are pregnant

Your initial reaction is likely to be one of shock. Your mind may play all sorts of tricks as it attempts to adapt to this new situation. It is not unusual for women to find themselves laughing or crying

Do You Want an Abortion?

when they least expect to, or feeling quite shaky inside, and unable to think clearly. This feeling will probably wear off quite quickly, and you will find that you can begin to work out what you want to do. You may experience a strange *distancing*, almost as though the pregnancy belongs to someone else. You may feel that you are in the middle of a bad dream which will go away when you wake up. Talking to others, whether it is to the doctor, or to friends and partner, often brings home the reality of your situation. If you have not told anyone, it is quite easy to delay seeking help because of this feeling that it is not really happening to you, and that it will somehow just go away if you wait long enough.

At the same time you may be experiencing some of the symptoms of early pregnancy, such as tiredness, queasiness, and feeling emotionally up and down. This can be a factor in coming to a decision. You need to decide which people, if any, should be involved. Partner, family or friends can be told, depending on your situation. In addition counsellors are available to listen and help, and so are doctors.

Talking to others

Talking to others is crucial in your decision-making. It is important that you do not take a decision like this alone, yet it can be hard to approach someone, either because you are afraid that they might betray your confidence or reject you or because you do not quite know what to say. Perhaps your pride makes it difficult, the feeling that as you got yourself into trouble, you should get yourself out. If you are anxious and upset, you may see your problem in an unrealistic way, and talking to others can help you see where you are wrong. Often it is in the process of explaining to someone else that you begin to see the issues more clearly; it is the questions asked that help, not the solutions offered by someone else.

When you talk to a friend allow yourself time, and starting with the time you became pregnant describe honestly what you felt at every stage. Do not be afraid to contradict yourself, because it is in the unravelling of the contradictions that you will understand exactly what you are feeling. Sometimes it helps to know what others felt under the same circumstances, but *your* feelings are more important.

Talking to friends, or counsellors, is different from talking to those closely involved. For example, *Sandra* felt 'I can't tell him. I know he wants me to have another child but I just don't want it. If I tell him I'm pregnant and want an abortion, he will be very upset and it will destroy our relationship. I do not want that; we get on great most of the time, and there is the little one to consider. I have told a pal and she has been great.'

Lynn was in an easier position. 'As soon as I got the result, Jim and I spoke about it a bit, and then decided to talk to my mum. She was angry at first, but calmed down and we all spoke about

Do You Want an Abortion?

it. Later she told me she was really pleased that we had been able to come to her.'

Linda was very isolated. She was 17 and became pregnant as a result of a holiday romance. 'I knew my mother would be really hurt, she does not believe in that sort of thing. Anyway, she has got enough on her plate with me dad. My pal has just had a wee boy and I can't talk to her. She would just want me to have it like she did.' Linda spoke to the doctor and a counsellor, both of whom were helpful. She did not tell anyone else and had to hide her feelings in front of those to whom she was closest. She found that it was comforting to talk to a counsellor who was right out of the situation, but understood what she was talking about.

Telling your partner or family is a matter of judgement. Pregnancy and abortion are big things to hide from your partner but in the end the only judge of the situation is you. As a general rule it is better to be as honest as you can in a relationship, because then you can be open about your feelings afterwards. The danger of not telling anyone is that you are not free to be yourself, you are always pretending to be happy or unconcerned, and yet you may be feeling quite desperate at times. On the other hand you may also enjoy a great sense of satisfaction at being solely in charge of your life.

Exploring the options

Exploring the options available can be harder than it sounds, but in making a good decision it is crucial. Think of yourself a year from hence and imagine that you *have had the baby*. What feelings arise? Are you scared, or do you quite like that picture? Your reaction will help you to know what you feel about the pregnancy. It will also make you look at the practical realities, such as where you would be living and where your money would be coming from. Would your partner be there, would it matter if he was not? Looking five years on, what would you foresee? Would it have all worked out for the best, or would you feel resentful at opportunities missed? Obviously you cannot know the answer completely, but from what you know of yourself, and what you have seen in the lives of others, you will probably be able to make a good guess.

Abortion

What do you think of *adoption*? Would that be a better option than being a single parent or terminating the pregnancy? The adoptive parents would be delighted, and your child would be well looked after. Could you cope with that? Would you always wonder about the child, would it be with sadness or a feeling that you did the right thing? What is *abortion* to you? Is it more important to consider the quality of the life to be led, by both mother and child, or the fact of life itself? Is it better to have an abortion than to have an unwanted child? Your religious background will affect your thinking, but in the end you may decide to follow your own beliefs rather than those of others. Can you live with your feelings afterwards, will you be upset, and do you have the necessary personal support to help you through? Even if you are seriously considering an abortion it is important to look at the other options available.

1) Continuing with the pregnancy and bringing up the child
The following people had good reason for anxiety about their pregnancies.

Jane was 16, and had known her boyfriend for two years, but was planning a nursing career. Her boyfriend wanted her to have the baby and her parents agreed to help her.

Do You Want an Abortion?

Penny was in her mid-thirties, divorced, with two school-age children: her partner was also divorced, with no children, and wanted this child. Penny had been offered a part-time job which suited her very well.

Julie was 22 and unemployed; she barely knew her partner, as they had met on holiday. She loved children and had the support of her mother.

Margaret was married, aged 40, with two teenage children. The pregnancy was an accident, and she and her husband were very shocked.

Doreen was 24, working, and engaged to be married. They had just put a deposit down on a house and relied on her income to pay for it.

Although these women continued with their pregnancies and looked after their children they could easily have chosen to seek an abortion. Julie was the only one of these five women who had no contact with the baby's father. Jane decided she was too young to marry, but included her boyfriend in her child's life; the others all stayed with their partners.

The role of the father is important, but hard to think about when the child is very young and does not really understand what it means to have a father. Later the problem becomes more complicated, especially when the child wants to know more about him. If you are thinking about having a child on your own it is perhaps important to consider that your child might have a contact with his/her father, even though you are no longer emotionally involved. Planning for this eventuality is better than being caught unprepared when either the father asks to see the child or the child to see the father.

The examples show that the support of their partners was as important as that of their families. When you are thinking whether you should continue with the pregnancy, particularly if you are planning to bring up the child on your own, you should think about who would be around to help you, if in need. Your needs and those of your child are closely entwined and if you feel alone and vulnerable it will affect your relationship with that child. Where will your money come from? *Jane* decided to look after the child for at least a year before resuming her studies and

Abortion

managed on social security. *Julie* did the same, though it changed her lifestyle very little as she had not been working before this happened.

Penny and her partner decided that as he had wanted the child so much he would alter his working in order to look after the child while Penny was working. *Margaret* stopped working in order to look after the child, but *Doreen* and her husband felt that they could not cope financially unless she worked. She took maternity leave and returned to full-time work using a childminder to care for the baby during the day.

If you decide to work then you have to think about who will care for the child while you are working. *Margaret* was quite clear that she would not hand her child over to anyone else. 'What is the point of having a child if all I do is hand it over to someone else?' *Doreen* did not like having a childminder, but felt it was better than giving up the house. This way she could give her child what she felt he should have, a decent home and enough money to buy clothes and toys. Many women feel that childminders can offer more to their children then they would be able to offer themselves if they were looking after the child all day. Your feelings about work and a career and your needs for self-fulfilment against what you think a child should have from its parents is a constant balancing act, both when the decision is taken and during the rest of the childhood.

Help from parents is very important but *Julie* relied on it too much. She and her mother found it hard to agree about disciplining the child, and at times he did not know whether to obey his mother or grandmother. Julie had left so much care to her mother that when she moved into her own flat, her son was very upset at leaving his Granny.

Although you may plan to have a child on your own, you will still have to face these issues.

Having a child brings responsibility and enjoyment. If you are a single parent you may find life rather a struggle, particularly if your income is low and your housing poor. It is harder to be tolerant of an active and demanding child if you are under stress, so it is important that you know how to deal with that stress, and get help from friends, family or professional people. Many single parents cope well and are pleased that they

Do You Want an Abortion?

decided to continue with the pregnancy. Others find it less easy to cope. In general the younger you are the harder it is, at least in the first few years. When you think about continuing the pregnancy consider whether you *want* the child, what are the practical issues, and can they be dealt with, and what do you expect of the father? If your parents are helping, what can you expect from them and what are your personal needs?

Up-to-date information about your housing rights and entitlement to State Benefits can be obtained from the following organisations:

> Citizens Advice Bureaux
>
> Child Poverty Action Group (CPAG)
>
> Shelter Housing Aid Centres
>
> Local DHSS offices
>
> Local Housing offices

Generally it is worth checking on your rights both with the official bodies such as DHSS and with advice agencies to ensure that you are told all that you need to know.

2) Adoption

This is probably the option you know least about, but you may have a very strong reaction to it. Adoption is often seen as giving away a child and this can seem a terrible thing to do. It is painful, but many see it as a mother taking a responsible decision to have her child cared for by someone who can offer it a much better life.

Children are placed for adoption by special adoption agencies or by particular social workers in a social services department. They vet couples who want to become adoptive parents and also arrange for children to be placed with these parents. If you are considering adoption you should contact either your local social services department or one of these agencies. Enquiring about adoption does not commit you to it; you can only give your consent to adoption, at the earliest, six weeks after the birth of

Abortion

the baby. It is not unusual for a woman to change her mind about adoption once the baby has been born. Your social worker will understand this and will help you, whatever your decision.

Before the baby is born you will see the social worker regularly in order to talk about adoption and how you want it to proceed. For instance, you might want the baby to leave hospital and if possible go straight to its prospective adopters. Alternatively, you might feel that you would want the baby placed with temporary foster parents so that you can have some time to make sure that you have made the right decision. You might feel that you would want to see the baby in hospital but not actually care for it, or that you would not want to see it at all, or you might want to care for it yourself in hospital. These preparations will ensure that your wishes are considered when you are in hospital.

It is helpful to begin to think about what sort of family you would want for your child. If you have strong religious views you might want the child brought up with respect for and knowledge of your religion. Physical characteristics can be important; for instance, if you are tall you may prefer your child to grow up in a family where at least some members of the family are tall; you might want your child placed with a family of similar racial origin to your own or you may feel that this is not important. Other things might be a priority: for instance, that with a well-educated or well-off family your child would have a better chance than you have had. On the other hand you may value friendliness and warmth more highly. The aim of this sort of discussion is to involve you in planning your child's future. It may be difficult to think in this way at first, but you will find that the social worker will do her or his best to help you.

After the baby is six weeks old the papers can be signed renouncing your parental rights. Some can make this decision at six weeks, others find they need more time; meanwhile the baby remains in foster care. If the social worker sees that the delay is not good for the baby, he or she will have to set a limit on the time you have for making the decision. In the end the social worker must act in the best interests of the child.

Adoptive parents recognise that it is important that the child knows that he/she is adopted from an early age, and therefore will at some stage wish to know about its natural mother. The social worker will have told them about you, and may have written something about you for reference later on. You may be able to write to your child giving information about yourself and your decision to place for adoption. This is often very valuable to the child as an indication of the care taken by you over the adoption.

Adoptive parents are often found by the same agency as employs the social workers, whom you see. Usually there are many more couples wanting to adopt than there are children available. The social workers talk with them about being a parent and in particular being the parent of someone else's child. They check up with the police and other agencies to see if the couple have anything known against them. It is ironic that prospective adoptive parents are much more carefully prepared for becoming parents than those who can have children naturally. Mistakes can be made but in general adoptive parents offer children a very good home.

You may worry that an adopted child could contact you later when he/she is an adult. When that child is sixteen in England, or seventeen in Scotland he/she can look at the original birth certificate, find your name and address and trace you in that way. In practice, many may check their mother's name, but few will go as far as tracing her; those that do, will often go via the agency who placed them in the first place and will be satisfied to know something about their mother. For details of local adoption agencies ask your local Citizens Advice Bureau, or look in the telephone directory or contact your local social services department.

Placing a child for adoption is not something that you are likely to forget. Many find it a painful memory, but feel that they did the right thing under the circumstances.

Understanding your feelings

Understanding your feelings is a crucial stage in making a decision or in coming to terms with the decision you have made. When you analyse how you feel you will find that you are

Abortion

reacting to the reason for your pregnancy and then to the pregnancy itself.

How did you become pregnant?

Your feelings may be influenced by the circumstances in which you became pregnant. Your pregnancy may be due to contraceptive failure; or to failure to use contraceptives, often for quite complicated reasons.

All contraceptive methods have a failure rate. With the combined pill it is very low, but you may have been given drugs which interfere with its effective action, without you realising it, or have been sick, had diarrhoea or missed taking some pills. The sheath and diaphragm have higher failure rates even if used properly. Occasionally some women become pregnant when the coil is still in place. If you are one of these women, you might feel that you were meant to be pregnant and continue with the pregnancy. It is more likely that if you are reading this book your reaction would be like *Rachel*'s: 'I took the pill because I didn't want to be pregnant, and I want an abortion; I don't want a child now.'

These women all became pregnant for reasons other than contraceptive failure:

Lindsay had known Duncan for some time and they had been having sex for about a year. She had been on the pill, but when she ran out of pills she did not return for more, and instead she and Duncan used sheaths but not every time. When Lindsay became pregnant she could not cope with a child. She explained that the more risks she took without becoming pregnant the more she worried that she might never be able to conceive.

Aileen was 22, and full of chatter. She went to a lot of parties and often got drunk. 'I've only had sex a few times, usually at parties, but I'm not really going steady with anyone, so I really don't think I should go on the pill.' Close relationships caused Aileen a lot of anxiety, especially when sexuality was involved; she dealt with this by showing that she was no prude and 'enjoyed herself' at parties, but without committing herself to anyone, thus avoiding possible rejection. Her need for comfort and affection would rise to the surface when drunk

Do You Want an Abortion?

and she would then be able to have a sexual relationship. She became pregnant after such a party, but did not want a child.

Usha was 19, and came from a fairly liberal Indian family. She had left home in order to study and met Paul, with whom there was a strong mutual attraction. 'My family would leave the choice of partner to me but they do not agree with sex before marriage and certainly do not talk about sex at home. What I know I learned from school.' She had been a bit uncertain about having a sexual relationship with Paul, but her feelings had been very strong and she missed the closeness of her family. She could not face coming to a clinic so he had used sheaths, but he stopped using them because he found them distasteful. Usha had been too shy to discuss contraception with him and she became pregnant.

Marion and George ended a long relationship, as they were always arguing. Marion threw away her pills and was adapting to seeing less of him when they met up again. They spent the evening together and had sex. Marion became pregnant; George denied it was his.

April and Fred were engaged, but he was away at sea for long periods of time. April was having a bad time at work and was feeling rather lonely, so when a male friend invited her out one evening she went and the evening ended with sex. Later April found herself pregnant. She commented 'I know it sounds silly, but I just didn't think it would happen to me.'

These pregnancies could have been avoided by sensible use of contraceptives. For each of them there was an underlying fear or anxiety which made it difficult. *Lindsay's* fear of infertility is very strong and very potent because fertility is so much a part of being female. Many women become pregnant in order to test their fertility and may even test it again after abortion. The fact that is makes no logical sense makes it all the more important that it is understood, because it has such an effect on how you behave.

Aileen and *Usha* had some similar problems expressed differently; both had considerable fears about sexual relationships. If you have been brought up to believe that you should not have sex outside marriage, but live in a culture where the opposite is expected, you are likely to be confused, especially if you are a bit unsure of yourself. *Usha* found herself in a passionate relationship at a time when she was entering a very new world and found it difficult to hold on to her family's values, especially in the context of strong sexual feeling.

Looking back, *Marion* felt very foolish about the pregnancy but said that it had all just happened, perhaps because they were used to having a sexual relationship and it had been one of the most enjoyable aspects of their relationship. She somehow did not think that having sex once could lead to pregnancy.

April was very upset at her pregnancy. She found it very hard to forgive herself for her betrayal and to understand that when things get difficult you tend to turn to someone else for comfort and that comfort and sex are quite closely linked.

For all these women understanding why they had become pregnant was important in coming to terms with an unwanted pregnancy and abortion. Accepting that they had a need for physical affection and comfort, which pulled them into risky situations, was particularly difficult.

Abortion on medical grounds

Perhaps you are pregnant by choice, but have discovered that the baby is abnormal, or damaged in some way, and the doctor has recommended that you have the pregnancy terminated. You will be in a very different situation from those described so far, because the baby may seem very real to you, and the loss all the greater. People may assume that you would be relieved to have an abortion and that there is little to discuss, and may not realise the dilemma you may be facing.

You may feel you could cope with a handicapped child, provided it is not too severely damaged, and may resent the assumption that you will want an abortion. Even if you are glad to be offered the choice, you will still have to face the pain of a late abortion. You may find that as the child was wanted or planned your feelings are more akin to the sadness following stillbirth. However, many of the other feelings described here might fit you.

Do You Want an Abortion?

How did you feel about the pregnancy?

The pivotal dilemma of abortion is the knowledge that your pregnancy is not wanted. You may have had children and have been happy to be pregnant, but this time you know that it is not right; or you may never have been pregnant but know that one day you would like children; possibly you never want to have children. You will be aware that for many people being pregnant is the confirmation of femininity, yet you are denying this part of you for very good reasons. It may be the first time you have had to ask yourself what you feel about being a parent, about what you feel a child needs at home, as well as what you hope to be able to give to the child. You will be trying to sort out what you could give to a child, as well as what you hope that a child will give to you.

Feelings about partner and pregnancy can swing wildly before settling into a more even pattern. This is why it is helpful to allow yourself *time* to be sure about your decision. Your reaction to the pregnancy when it is first diagnosed may be to feel that you want an abortion. That feeling may not change, but even after two or three days it will be a more clearly thought-out decision, in part because you will have accepted to some extent the reality that you are pregnant. Some will change their minds several times before coming to a decision. Women who have had their abortions performed very soon after the diagnosis of pregnancy sometimes feel that they did not have time to think, that it was all too quick, and may regret it.

Blame

It seems to be a basic human reaction to try and apportion *blame* and there is a limited choice when it comes to pregnancy. Often you will swing from blaming yourself to blaming your partner, before recognising the reality of the situation. *Lisa* expressed this very clearly. 'After I had had sex with him, I felt that I had made a mistake and he was not the sort of man I really wanted. I felt angry with myself for being taken in by him. Now looking back, I can see that he was pretty inexperienced as well, and did not have much idea of what to do himself.' Given this situation, Lisa was quite glad that her partner did not know of the pregnancy because she could make all the decisions herself.

Abortion

When you *blame yourself* and say 'I should have said "no" to him', you are correct in that if you had said no you would not have become pregnant. However, you are also colluding with the belief that it is the woman alone who should say no and take responsibility for the consequences of having sex, not the man. It is a variation of the double standard that says men should sow their wild oats but women should remain pure. It denies the reality of a mutually-caring union.

Taking all the blame for the pregnancy means that you also take control, and ensure that the decision is yours. The danger is that if you take all the blame you can also carry all the negative feelings alone. For instance, if you feel it is really all your fault you may think you should be punished for your sin. The sin might be having had a sexual relationship, or it might be considering abortion. Punishment absolves you; once you are punished you can get on with your life. Often it is harder to be treated with tolerance when you feel this way; you can feel obscurely cheated if no one has given you a hard time. You may even look for punishment elsewhere.

In reality you are responsible for the pregnancy, but so is your partner; carrying all the blame is unrealistic, even untrue. It may help you cope in the short run, but carrying all the blame for an unwanted pregnancy can leave you feeling worse about yourself than is necessary.

There are times when it is quite clear where the blame lies, as when one half of the partnership hoped that the pregnancy would shore up a shaky relationship as in the following situations:

> 'He had often talked about children so when things got difficult between us I thought I would get pregnant. I decided that having a child would hold us together, hold his attention.'

> 'He knew I wanted to leave him, so one night he threw away my diaphragm and forced me to have sex. He was sure I would never have the guts to have an abortion against his will.'

Do You Want an Abortion?

Men also blame women for the pregnancy even when it is logically not their fault. Eric felt that his girlfriend, who had a coil, had become pregnant in order to trap him into marriage. He found it hard to believe that it was simply a method failure. She had an abortion because his reaction was so extreme that she felt it would be unfair to have a child under these circumstances.

Anger

You are likely to feel *angry* when your partner has clearly used you. *Jane* commented, 'He was all over me until he got what he wanted. He said he would be careful. When I told him that his care had made me pregnant he didn't say anything and I haven't seen him since.' Sometimes you will want to blame your partner rather than face up to your part in what happened: this is not helpful because in the future you will continue to avoid responsibility for what happens to you.

Sadly, if you are a victim of rape or incest you may feel so violated and invaded that you carry the burden of guilt and distress, for the attack and the pregnancy. It is very important to be able to turn the anger away from yourself on to the attacker where it belongs. If you were mugged you would not blame yourself. Rape and incest are violent sexual attacks and are not the fault of the victim.

Anger is a powerful emotion and is present in all of us. If it is misdirected it is dangerous; turned inwards, it can be an important factor in depression; turned outwards it can hurt others unless it is managed carefully. If it is used constructively it can be a potent force for change and development.

Guilt

Guilt is different from self-blame because it carries the strong implication of sin — sin at having a sexual relationship, especially outside marriage, or sin at considering abortion. You may be like *Ann*, a Catholic, who found help from a sympathetic priest. 'He listened to what I had said and we talked about penitence and absolution and he helped me a great deal.' Or you may be like *Irene* who said 'I can't justify abortion, but I can't do anything else.' Looking at guilt is part of taking seriously what you are doing in having an abortion, whether you see it as essentially ending a life, or as simply cleaning away a mass of cells.

Self-blame and *guilt* are both negative and positive in their effects. If you are left feeling worthless and bad inside you can become seriously depressed. If however they become a spur to change, to re-evaluating your behaviour, to accepting yourself as you really are, then they can be beneficial.

Knowing and listening to your feelings

Your feelings will change during the time between knowing you are pregnant and having an abortion, depending on whom you have spoken to, time, and your day-to-day situation. You may feel angry at your partner one day and the next day blame yourself, but usually feelings begin to settle down after a few days. This process can be greatly helped by people who are prepared to listen constructively to what you are saying and not judge you.

Rebecca described how disgusted she felt at being pregnant and how she wanted to hide away so that no one should know of the pregnancy. She had become pregnant by a man she hardly knew after a one-night stand. She was recently separated from her husband and was looking after her two school-age children. It was the first time for months that she had had a night out and it had ended in disaster, leaving her feeling that she had let herself down. She felt her only option was abortion, and was shocked that she felt so cold about it. Abortion had always meant to her immorality, callousness and irresponsibility. Talking to the counsellor was helpful because she did not judge her but rather could see how vulnerable Rebecca had been in her need for some attention for herself. Recognising her own needs as well as those of her children allowed Rebecca to plan realistically for a future in which she was entitled to care and affection. For Rebecca, understanding why she had behaved as she did was *not* a justification for wanting an abortion but a help in avoiding a similar situation in the future.

Maybe you have an overwhelming feeling that you want to be rid of the pregnancy and yet you are aware how callous such a reaction must seem to an outsider. Such feelings can be a way of

Do You Want an Abortion?

distancing yourself from the pregnancy and not facing up to conflicting feelings; but it can also be a simple indicator of your fear of having that child. Rather than fighting such a reaction, it is better to ask yourself why you feel so strongly against your pregnancy. Does it seem to be a trap keeping you in a relationship you do not want, or doubt? Would having a child prevent you from doing what seems most important to you? Are your feelings related to how you felt about your own parents and your childhood? Answers to these questions might help you understand more clearly underlying anxieties in your life and will make your reasons for your decision more understandable.

Sometimes it is very hard to come to a decision. Abortion, adoption, or bringing up the child can seem equally difficult. There are no easy answers. You will have to make the best of a bad job, which may seem very unsatisfactory. Sometimes it is a question of finding out what you definitely do not want and taking your decision from there. *Karen* was quite undecided about her pregnancy. She was 35, happily married, and working. She had avoided thinking about having a child to the point where she almost denied the possibility. She used the diaphragm conscientiously but became pregnant. There was some upheaval in her life at the time and Karen felt that abortion was the best option, even though her husband felt they might be able to manage.

She was given her hospital appointment and checked in, but left after an hour. She and her husband discussed it again, she decided on abortion, she went to hospital and left after two hours. Karen still talked about it but simply could not bring herself to have an abortion: she continued with the pregnancy almost by default.

Vanessa was entirely different. She was ambitious but unemployed. She was not happy on the pill and though her partner usually used sheaths, they took a risk one night and as a result she became pregnant. There were some professional openings likely in the future, but she found that she was torn between feeling that there was no way she could have a child and the hope that a child might fill the emptiness of her life. At the same time she felt that was not a good enough reason to have a child. She eventually decided on abortion.

Abortion

Ambivalence is not easily resolved, but talking it over is important and writing down what you feel can be very helpful as you can look back later on and remember how you came to your decision. You may look back and say 'If I had known what I know now I would have behaved differently.' But you can only act on what you know at the time and you may always have doubts, however fleeting or slight.

Your partner's role

You are pregnant, you will have to have the child, or go through abortion, or place the child for adoption. If you have the child you will very often have to carry the main responsibility for child care, yet you could not have become pregnant without a man. The usual picture of family life includes men, they are half the human race. What should their role be in abortion?

Some men make their views quite clear by denying that the pregnancy has anything to do with them, or by simply removing themselves from the scene. Whatever their motives, whether it be fear of responsibility or panic because they are not sure what is expected of them, there is little you can do. Not all men are like this; many have very strong feelings about children and may want them more than their partners. If they care about their partners, they may want to be involved, even if the relationship has ended; many will feel that they should help even if they do not want the child or a relationship with the woman.

The power is with women; men cannot prevent a woman from having an abortion nor can they force one on them. Some men try to bully their partner to do what they want, but there are a lot of men who are very uncertain what to do. Often they wish they could be the ones going through the trauma, but as they cannot, they have to sit by and help. It is hard under these circumstances to accept that listening and looking after is as important as more dramatic actions. Just as women need to *look at* how they feel, men need to *know* how women feel. In close relationships it may be important for the woman to know what her partner thinks she should do, but he should not attempt to impose it on her. Women can be as frustrated and angry with a man who refuses to say what he wants, in the name of tolerance and letting her decide, as with a man who insists that his way is the only way.

Facing the crisis of an unexpected pregnancy can make or break a relationship between two people. Listening, understanding, and caring for each other can make it possible to get through the difficulties.

Conclusion

Whether abortion is a straightforward decision, or is agonisingly difficult, looking carefully at all the options, considering the risks and being honest with yourself about how you feel, will ensure that your choice is the best under the circumstances. Understanding why you became pregnant can help you avoid another unwanted pregnancy by seeing when you are likely to be at risk. You may feel that you will never have another sexual relationship and therefore do not wish to think about contraception. Sometimes this is a way of punishing yourself for your sexuality, which led you to an unwanted pregnancy and abortion. Sexual feelings are a part of you, whether they are strong or weak, and can be a source of great pleasure and comfort in your life. Consideration of pregnancy and what it would mean should be an integral part of a heterosexual relationship, but it should not interfere with its enjoyment.

4. Can You Have an Abortion?

The law, what does it say?

The 1967 Abortion Act states that: '...a person shall not be guilty of an offence under the law relating to abortion when a pregnancy is terminated by a registered medical practitioner, if two registered medical practitioners are of the opinion formed in good faith —

(a) that the continuance of the pregnancy would involve risk to the life of the pregnant woman, or of injury to the physical or mental health of the pregnant woman or any existing children of her family, greater than if the pregnancy were terminated; ... and account may be taken of the pregnant woman's actual or reasonably forseeable environment.

   or

(b) that there is substantial risk that if the child were born it would suffer from such physical or mental abnormalities as to be seriously handicapped.'

The law, what does it mean?

Abortion is legal under certain circumstances. Firstly, where it is necessary to save the woman's life. This is for women suffering from conditions such as acute cancer (particularly of the breast) or acute heart disease where pregnancy may cause death. Women who are likely to commit suicide because of an unwanted pregnancy can also be helped under this part of the Act. Secondly, where continuing the pregnancy is likely to cause greater physical or mental damage to the woman or to her children or family than would having an abortion. Because pregnancy causes more women to suffer physical or mental harm than abortions do, most women who are distressed because of an unwanted pregnancy may have an abortion on these grounds. Thirdly, abortion is legal where there is evidence that the child is likely to be born with a serious physical or mental disability.

Unwanted pregnancy

The Abortion Act makes it legal for doctors to agree to an abortion for any woman who is distressed by an unwanted pregnancy. The source of her distress may include her social circumstances as part of her mental health and well-being. The law allows the doctor to take into account the woman's family circumstances both during the pregnancy and those likely to arise if the baby was born. However, doctors vary in their interpretation of the law and, of course, in their views on abortion.

Doctors who are opposed to abortion

There is a conscientious objection clause in the Abortion Act which allows doctors to refuse help to a woman seeking abortion unless her life is at risk from the pregnancy. A woman's request for advice and treatment may therefore be refused if the doctor objects to abortion on moral and religious grounds. Roman Catholics in particular are resolutely opposed to any law which, in their opinion, allows the killing of a human life. Not all churches are opposed to abortion, though. Anglican churches in England, the Jewish faith, the Methodists and many other free churches support the 1967 Abortion Act.

Some doctors who are opposed to abortion argue that modern medical techniques are now so well developed that the risks during pregnancy are minimal and cannot and should not be compared unfavourably with the risks associated with abortion. These doctors refuse to accept that social or mental factors should carry any weight.

Abortion

Some women who have had an abortion

A young mother who already had three children went to see her GP about being sterilised. Examination revealed that she was already pregnant. Feeling totally unable to cope emotionally or financially with another child she requested and was referred for abortion.

A student discovered she was pregnant in her final term at college. Although she felt she would eventually like to have children she was extremely distressed by this unplanned pregnancy. Her college doctor helped her with her request for termination of the pregnancy.

A 16-year-old schoolgirl didn't think anything of it when she began to miss her periods. They had been irregular and she had been having occasional 'spotting'. When she also began to feel sick and have sore breasts she decided to go to a Brook Centre for a pregnancy test. The examination revealed that she was already 12 weeks pregnant. Her mother supported her decision to terminate the pregnancy. She was referred to a local hospital by the Brook Centre.

How late in pregnancy?

The Abortion Act doesn't mention a time limit for abortion. Instead this is defined in the Infant Life Preservation Act (of 1929) which says that it is an offence to abort a foetus which is capable of being born alive. At the moment the Act sets 28 weeks as the critical age at which a foetus is considered capable of independent life. In practice, because of possible error in determining age, this meant that the limit for abortion was usually 26 weeks. But in August 1985 there was considerable pressure from the medical profession for the government to change the limit to 24 weeks. Scientific advance has meant a greater likelihood of keeping foetuses younger than 28 weeks alive outside the womb. In the event a change in the law did not happen. Instead the Minister for Health obtained an agreement from abortion service providers that they would not terminate pregnancies of more than 24 weeks.

In fact very few late abortions are carried out. In 1984, only about 13% of abortions were between 12 and 20 weeks. Most abortions are before 12 weeks and only 2% are after 20 weeks. It is difficult to get an NHS abortion after 12 weeks in most areas of the country.

What happens if you're under 16?

Anyone over the age of 16 has the right to consent to any medical treatment. A girl under 16 may have sufficient maturity and understanding to give her own consent to treatment. Otherwise she will need to obtain the consent of her parent or guardian. Good medical practice would, however, require a doctor in most cases to seek involvement of the parents before agreeing to carry out an abortion on someone under 16.

What happens if you live in Northern Ireland?

The 1967 Abortion Act doesn't extend to Northern Ireland so a woman cannot obtain an abortion unless her life is at risk. Pregnancy counselling is available from the Ulster Pregnancy Advisory Association, 719a Lisburn Road, Belfast, BT9 6GU. Tel: Belfast 667345. They can then refer you to BPAS in Liverpool. The usual fee applies.

What happens if you live in the Republic of Ireland?

Abortion is illegal in Eire. Irish women can obtain pregnancy counselling from the Well Woman Centre, 60 Eccles Street, Dublin 1 (Tel: Dublin 728051/381365) or 63 Lower Leeson Street, Dublin 2 (Tel: Dublin 789366/789504).

Abortion

IN CONFIDENCE   **Certificate A**

Not to be destroyed within three years of the date of operation

ABORTION ACT 1967

Certificate to be completed before an abortion is performed under Section 1(1) of the Act

I, ...
(Name and qualifications of practitioner in block capitals)

of ....
....
(Full address of practitioner)

Have/have not* seen/and examined* the pregnant woman to whom this certificate relates at ....
....
(Full address of place at which patient was seen or examined)

on ....

and I ....
....
(Name and qualifications of practitioner in block capitals)

of ....
....
(Full address of practitioner)

Have/have not* seen/and examined* the pregnant woman to whom this certificate relates at ....
....
(Full address of place at which patient was seen or examined)

on ....

We hereby certify that we are of the opinion, formed in good faith, that in the case of ....
(Full name of pregnant woman in block capitals)

of ....
....
(Usual place of residence of pregnant woman in block capitals)

(Ring appropriate number(s))

1. the continuance of the pregnancy would involve risk to the life of the pregnant woman greater than if the pregnancy were terminated;
2. the continuance of the pregnancy would involve risk of injury to the physical or mental health of the pregnant woman greater than if the pregnancy were terminated;
3. the continuance of the pregnancy would involve risk of injury to the physical or mental health of the existing child(ren) of the family of the pregnant woman greater than if the pregnancy were terminated;
4. there is substantial risk that if the child were born it would suffer from such physical or mental abnormalities as to be seriously handicapped.

This certificate of opinion is given before the commencement of the treatment for the termination of pregnancy to which it refers and relates to the circumstances of the pregnant woman's individual case.

Signed ....

Date ....

Signed ....

*Delete as appropriate
FORM H.S.A. 1
Dd 8405531 300M 6/83 Ed(209595)

Date ....

Abortion in practice — who will help?

Although the Abortion Act says that a woman needs two doctors' opinions before being able to have an abortion, the first doctor will usually organise the second for you. Both have to sign the 'green form' (in England and Wales) or 'Certificate A' (in Scotland) to give details of the woman's legal grounds for abortion (see p. 42). You don't need to see this form but you will almost certainly hear it mentioned. The first doctor may be a GP, a doctor in a family planning clinic or youth advisory centre, a private doctor or a doctor in a private abortion clinic, such as one of the abortion charities. The second doctor is usually the one who performs the operation but that need not necessarily be so.

Family doctor

Some people feel straightaway that their doctor will be able to help. For others he or she is the last person with whom they would want to discuss an unwanted pregnancy. Some women are afraid to even approach their GP, anticipating an unsympathetic or even hostile reception. Many women feel they simply don't want to talk with their GP about abortion. Apart from the anguish of an unwanted pregnancy, discussing anything even remotely to do with sex and relationships is never easy. You may feel it's especially difficult if the GP has known you since childhood and you feel he or she hasn't got used to treating you as an adult. You could always try asking for a referral after briefly explaining the problem. Try asking the GP's receptionist for advice. She (or he) may be able to suggest that although your doctor would be unhelpful, another doctor in the practice is likely to be more supportive. Since you don't need to say your name or address over the phone, your privacy is not at risk. The telephone is a useful way of finding out information anonymously and you can always call back later to make the appointment. It is quite usual to see another GP in the same practice other than the one you're registered with. You can also

Abortion

go to an entirely separate GP in another practice. You may have a friend or know of someone whose GP was particularly helpful. Whatever happens with your GP, remember that all consultations are confidential. If your doctor immediately turns down your request for abortion, then asking for a referral elsewhere is probably not worthwhile. Doctors with religious or other conscientious objection to abortion are likely to be unwilling to help at all.

If your doctor refuses, try to ask for the reason. If the reason for refusal is a medical one, then you may try asking for a second opinion. The doctor doesn't have to agree to arrange this for you. Changing your doctor or going straight to a family planning clinic, Brook Centre or abortion charity may be the only way of getting one.

Clinics and advice centres

Family planning clinics may be able to refer you for an abortion, especially if you are registered with them and your pregnancy is the result of failed contraception. Again, a receptionist could tell you over the phone about the welcome to expect and perhaps even which doctors to avoid. Many family planning clinics run youth advisory sessions people under 25.

Brook Advisory Centres all offer pregnancy counselling and will try to help with referral for abortion through the NHS. Although primarily intended for people under 25, Brook will try to help anyone of any age with an unwanted pregnancy (see p 81 for addresses).

Other *Youth Advisory Centres* (e.g. the London Youth Advisory Centre — 26 Prince of Wales Road, London NW5 3LG, tel: 01-267 4792) also offer pregnancy counselling and referral for abortion as well as pregnancy testing. Some youth advisory centres don't have medical members of staff so can't do pregnancy testing or abortion referral. They would undoubtedly be a good source of information, advice and counselling.

Women's Centres often do pregnancy testing. They're a good source of information about local services.

Citizens Advice Bureaux keep information on local birth control services or you could try the local student centre.

Abortion charities

The abortion charities such as British Pregnancy Advisory Service (BPAS), Pregnancy Advisory Service (PAS) and Marie Stopes all help women faced with a problem pregnancy. They provide a complete service including pregnancy testing, counselling, and consultation with 2 doctors who will sign the 'green form' or certificate A; all this can usually be arranged within the first visit. They will also offer an abortion follow-up appointment and advice on future contraception. You will be referred to a private nursing home for the abortion. All the abortion charities would certainly be helpful and supportive.

Abortion

You're guaranteed a minimum of delay. Expect only from a few days to a week from the first consultation to the operation. They all charge a similar fee which is around £150 if you are less than 12 weeks pregnant, £165 for between 14 and 18 weeks pregnant and £230 for over 22 weeks pregnant. The charities will always try to help. They may be able to work out a payment plan for you if the fee is a difficult financial burden.

BPAS has branches throughout Britain, and nursing homes in Warwickshire, South Yorkshire, Bournemouth, Liverpool and Brighton (see p. 81 for addresses).

PAS have 2 branches in London; they refer women to their nursing home in Richmond (see p. 81).

Marie Stopes has only one location in London (see p. 81). They refer women to one of several nursing homes in the London area.

Why go to a charity?

There are two main reasons. For the majority of women it's because the NHS was unable to help. The other reason is also to do with failings in the NHS. A woman may have an appointment for an NHS abortion but decide that the waiting time is unacceptable. Some women feel that they're able to find the money or are willing to borrow if it means having the abortion quickly. A third more unusual reason is because of confidentiality. For people such as nurses, who work in their local gynaecology wards, running into colleagues may be a problem. All abortion facilities will be concerned to protect your privacy. Anyway, in NHS gynae wards you could be there for all sorts of reasons.

Private abortion organisations (non-charities)

There are some private clinics who do abortions. Because they are profit-making, they often charge quite high fees. All abortion clinics have to have a licence to operate so they are unlikely to be unsafe or have lower standards than anywhere else.

Can You Have an Abortion?

Will you be able to get an NHS abortion?

Although you should be realistic about your chances of getting an NHS abortion, don't discount the possibility in the first instance. Ask around, talk to friends, phone up your local family planning clinic or advice centre; they should know about local services. Don't be put off. The Abortion Act does not oblige hospitals or doctors to provide services but government working parties and select committees have said that women should not be forced to seek help in the private sector.

Nobody should ever try to induce abortion themselves. Don't listen to myths about gin and hot water. They don't work, they are illegal, and they're likely to make you very ill.

Getting an abortion can be full of pitfalls and problems. But, try not to be discouraged. The problems are unlikely to be of your making. A recent report pointed to delays and inefficiencies in NHS abortion services. Many are due to lack of funding, some to lack of organisation; others are certainly caused by people within the system who are opposed to abortion and therefore aren't concerned to make the services adequate or efficient.

It is difficult to get an abortion on the NHS if you are more than 12 weeks pregnant. Unfortunately waiting lists at some hospitals or clinics mean that women referred by their doctors at 10 or even 8 weeks may then have to wait 3 or 4 weeks by which time they are over the hospital's limit and so are refused.

Some hospitals or clinics don't want to help women who've already had more than one abortion.

Almost all hospitals and clinics operate strict rules refusing to help anyone living outside a given catchment area (which in some cases does not coincide with the health authority area).

Some hospitals and clinics have strange administrative quirks which can cause delays. A North London hospital for example will only make appointments for abortion patients between 9 and 9.30 on a Monday morning. For those who don't get through, there's another week to wait and then no guarantee of an appointment.

Agency arrangements

In order to improve services some health authorities have made 'agency arrangements' with local private abortion agencies. Sometimes they are with one of the abortion charities, otherwise with a private non-charity. Under these agreements, the NHS pays for the woman to have her abortion in the private sector. The system works well where there is resistance to abortion from local NHS gynaecologists. A woman can have a free abortion from a specialist group with assurance of understanding and support. Practitioners who are opposed to abortion are not responsible for running the service. Women seeking abortion feel anxious enough without having to deal with hostility and prejudice.

Where agency schemes exist they are usually administered by the local authority and mostly require referral from a GP. Even if you approach a family planning clinic or Brook Centre about abortion you may be advised that referral through the NHS via an agency arrangement can only be through your GP.

Overall, persevere and don't delay. As soon as you think you might be pregnant be ready to start tackling the system. Try to get a good source of advice and don't be afraid. Despite the system being difficult, there are a great many people who understand how you feel and will want to offer support.

What happens when you see the doctor?

Wherever you go for help with abortion, whether to your family doctor, youth advisory centre or abortion charity, there are certain formalities which always happen. The doctor will examine you to make sure you are pregnant and determine by how many weeks. You will then need to explain how you feel about the pregnancy and why you want an abortion. Before the doctor can agree to refer you for abortion, he or she needs to fully understand your reasons and to be convinced that you have legal grounds. Depending on the skill and interest of the doctor, you may find this discussion very useful in coming to terms with your own decision about the pregnancy. If you go to a Brook Centre or anywhere with a counsellor you may be able to continue your discussion about your feelings with the counsellor. If you haven't gone to such a centre, and the doctor is too busy to spend a long time with you, it may be a good idea to seek counselling elsewhere. You may be uneasy about discussing any doubts or conflicting feelings you have with your doctor. Many women feel they have to convince the doctor that they are sure of the decision in order to enlist help and support in obtaining abortion referral. You may decide that *once you have the doctor's agreement* to support your request for abortion, then is the best time to arrange counselling.

5. What Does Abortion Involve?

What happens with the second doctor?

Some common experiences are expressed by these three women who all eventually had an abortion within the NHS.

'He was very nice. He spent quite a lot of time talking with me about what would happen. He answered the questions I had and made me feel that he understood.'

'I felt like I had committed a crime and he was dangling my fate in front of me. When he said no he couldn't help I felt as though I had been hit in the face.'

'Guilt was my biggest problem. I knew I'd made the right decision. They agreed to help but seemed so reluctant. The gynaecologist made me feel like a naughty child.'

After seeing the first doctor in your local practice, family planning clinic or youth advisory centre, you will be given an appointment to see a consultant gynaecologist at a hospital or clinic. This appointment should be made for you during your consultation with the first doctor, or you will be asked to phone in later for the precise date and time, or it will be sent to you by post. Watch out for time passing. If you haven't heard within a few days phone the doctor and ask about the delay. The appointment will usually be within three weeks of your being seen by the first doctor. If you will be more than 12 weeks pregnant by the time of the appointment, check with the first doctor that this is not too late.

What Does Abortion Involve?

With the abortion charities the procedure is probably different; the second doctor will normally be available to talk with you during your first visit. So most of what follows is to do with the procedure in the NHS. Hospital gynaecologists vary considerably in the amount of time they will spend with you. Most will want to go over why you feel you want to have an abortion. They too must sign the form acknowledging your legal grounds for abortion. Some will discuss with you the nature of the operation, precisely what will happen and how you're likely to feel afterwards. Others will not go into details but merely ask if you understand the nature of the operation and are sure you want it. He or she will examine you to determine the stage of pregnancy. You may even be asked to have a scan if there is uncertainty about the number of weeks pregnant you are. (An ultrasonic scan enables the doctor to see the developing foetus on a screen so that the stage of pregnancy can be checked accurately.)

As long as the gynaecologist agrees to your request for termination of pregnancy he or she will complete the green form or certificate A and give you a date for the operation. Most family doctors, or doctors in family planning clinics and Brook Centres, would not refer you to a hospital gynaecologist unless they had first made sure that your request would be treated with respect and sympathy. Nevertheless there are times when a gynaecologist will refuse to help a woman seeking abortion. The reason may be a medical one. It may be entirely practical. For example, there may be only ten beds a week available for abortion but 20 women a week seeking the operation. If the gynaecologist does refuse, immediately go back to the first doctor and explain what has happened. He or she will be able to make enquiries for you and occasionally, by discussing your special circumstances with the gynaecologist, change the decision. Whatever the reasons for refusal, you will probably want to know. If you weren't told or were too upset to ask, the first doctor will be able to find out for you.

If you feel sure you want to continue seeking abortion, the first doctor should be able to suggest an alternative course of action. You could ask for a second opinion. Otherwise you might consider going to one of the abortion charities, especially if the reason you were turned away by the NHS gynaecologist was lack of available appointments or because you were too late on in pregnancy to comply with the hospital regulations or the gynaecologist's views.

The way you are treated by the hospital or clinic doctor may seriously affect your feelings about abortion. Try talking to a friend or your partner about any of the consultations you have. Again a counsellor will be able to help you deal with hostile or indifferent remarks from health professionals. Try not to take anything too much to heart. Often gynaecologists are overburdened and bound by hospital rules. Nevertheless there is no excuse for rudeness or insulting remarks. And, if you feel you've been badly treated, your local community health council will help you make a complaint. Their address will certainly be in the telephone directory and listed with your local Citizens Advice Bureau.

The abortion appointment

Make sure that the date you are given for the *operation* does not make you more than 12 weeks pregnant. If it does then point this out to the hospital or clinic doctor. Ask if the operation can still be done after 12 weeks. If not then try to get an earlier date. If you were promised notification of the date for the abortion by post, wait for a few days then contact the hospital or clinic and make sure you haven't been overlooked. Ask why there has been a delay.

What does the abortion operation involve?

The kind of operation you have and how much time it takes depends on:

- how pregnant you are

- facilities at the hospital or clinic

- where you live in relation to the hospital or clinic.

What Does Abortion Involve?

Most abortions take very little time, 10 or 15 minutes at the most. But, because they are usually done under general anaesthetic, the whole procedure, including recovery time, can take several hours. In some cases you will be asked to stay overnight, as complications may develop in the hours immediately following the operation. If you go to a day care unit, you will only be asked to stay overnight if you need to travel for more than 2 hours. Day care facilities for abortion are available in only a few places in the country. The 2-hour restriction also applies with the abortion charities. Whether you have your abortion privately or with the NHS and whether or not you think you'll need to spend the night, you will need to take an overnight bag with a nightgown, dressing-gown and toiletries. If it turns out that you can leave a few hours after the abortion there must be someone to collect you and to spend the night with you.

If you have travelled a long way for an abortion, such as from Spain, the Irish Republic or Northern Ireland, there are organisations who offer 'a friend' to help with practical problems. Accommodation for a couple of days after the abortion, for example, can be a difficulty and expensive. Many women will prefer not to immediately have to face a journey home. To find out about this possibility see page 83.

Being admitted

'Once I was there, at the hospital, I wished myself anywhere else in the world. The woman in the next bed was crying, and the nurse seemed very formal. She asked me about my marital status. I felt so ashamed.'

'It was like being on a conveyor belt, you felt that these people knew what they were doing, and their obvious competence was quite reassuring.'

'The porters were great, I can't remember now what it was, but they made a joke. I felt drowsy and sad, but there I was laughing.'

The gynaecologist or a clerk will have given you details of the ward in the hospital or clinic and the time you should be there.

Abortion

Try not to be late. The ward sister or clerk will admit you — that is, your name and address will be ticked off on a list. Someone will then go through a few personal details and do a brief medical check usually including taking your temperature and blood pressure. You will be asked to undress and get into bed. In some hospitals and clinics you are admitted the day before the abortion but in many places you are admitted the same day.

An hour or so before the operation you will be given an injection (or sometimes a pill) to make you feel drowsy; this is the pre-med. Porters will come and help you on to a trolley. In the anteroom before the operating theatre, or sometimes in the theatre itself, you will be given the anaesthetic. This is usually given by an injection into a vein on the back of your hand.

In some day care units and often at the abortion charities, if you are less than 12 weeks pregnant you may be asked if you would prefer a *local anaesthetic*. This is put into the cervix, doesn't hurt very much, but it means that you will be conscious during the whole procedure. The advantages of local anaesthetic are that there will be fewer physical side effects and a shorter recovery time. You may feel that being conscious throughout is a big disadvantage. Sometimes there are medical reasons for not giving a general anaesthetic.

If you practise deep breathing exercises before the operation and can get someone to hold your hand (some places will allow your partner or a friend to stay with you) you may find local anaesthetic very acceptable. Deep breathing can help you to remain calm and you will be glad to have the whole procedure over with quickly.

Abortions before 12-14 weeks (first trimester abortion)

Most abortions are carried out before 12 weeks of pregnancy and the commonest method is called *vacuum aspiration* or suction. It can be done under local or general anaesthetic. There are 2 stages. First, the cervix is dilated or widened by carefully introducing a series of thin rods (called *sounds*) of increasing size,

What Does Abortion Involve?

in and out of your cervix one at a time. Once the cervix has widened — just a few millimetres — a tube is introduced into the uterus (womb) through the cervix. The contents of the womb are then sucked out using a suction apparatus attached to the tube.

If you have a local anaesthetic you will be able to see the instruments used, unless you prefer to keep your eyes closed or perhaps to meditate throughout. You may experience some discomfort rather like bad period cramps but that's all. The most disconcerting part will be the noise of the suction.

> 'The nurse held my hand. I remember hers were warm and soft, her concern made me want to cry. She talked gently about what was happening, and breathed slowly and deeply to help me feel calm.'

Another common method of abortion used, instead of vacuum aspiration, between 12 and 14 weeks of pregnancy is *Dilation and Curettage*, or *D and C*. It is almost always done under general anaesthetic but doesn't have to be.

The cervix is widened in the same way as for vacuum aspiration. Sometimes this part of the procedure is aided by inserting prostaglandin pessaries or a substance called Laminaria (a kind of seaweed) into the vagina. Either technique can help the cervix to open easily and may reduce any risk of damage caused by the metal sounds. In D and C the contents of the womb are then removed by an instrument called a curette rather than by suction. The curette is made of soft wire and looks like a pan scourer. It is used to gently clean out the womb.

Occasionally a doctor may combine vacuum aspiration and D and C if it seems that suction has not completely removed the contents of the womb. At 12 weeks of pregnancy the foetus is only about 50 mm long (the size of a thumbnail), and most of the tissue removed during abortion is the afterbirth (placenta) and blood. The amount is rather like a very heavy period.

How do you feel just afterwards?

> 'When I woke up I felt so relieved and optimistic about the future. I slept for a while; I felt a bit delicate, and had the

Abortion

> occasional cramping pain. When I went to the toilet it hurt a bit, but the next day I felt well. It was great not to wake up feeling sick. That's when I knew I wasn't pregnant any more.'

> 'When I woke up I just cried and cried. I didn't know exactly what it was about. When my boyfriend came to collect me, he looked so worried and I was so pleased to see him that I stopped crying. I felt much better then. I haven't really felt upset since.'

A general anaesthetic may cause you to feel a little sick on waking. You may feel drowsy for a couple of hours after you regain consciousness. Take your time, don't try to get up immediately. When you begin to walk around you may feel some cramping in your lower abdomen. This is quite usual. You will probably bleed for a couple of days after the abortion so make sure to have a supply of sanitary towels and take some with you to the hospital or clinic. If the bleeding persists and is very heavy you should see a doctor immediately. Your next period should happen within about 6 weeks of the abortion. If it does not appear, go back to see the doctor.

Sometimes the abortion will not have completely removed all the contents of the womb and you will experience cramps and bleeding because of the retained products. If this happens, it's usually in the first few days following abortion. You should immediately return to the doctor and will probably have to have a D and C. Retained products can sometimes lead to an infection; you might just have a temperature or you may get bleeding and pain as well. If this happens it's usually about a week to 10 days after the abortion. You should see a doctor, as you may need an antibiotic.

Aftercare

> 'I just walked out of the hospital and caught a bus home. I felt OK, but a bit strange. Everyone else was going home as usual, and I had just come out of hospital after an abortion. It was all rather unreal. I looked at those people and wondered what they would think if they knew.'

What Does Abortion Involve?

Make sure you look after youself. Relax and take only light exercise for a couple of weeks. If you have small children, try and get your partner or a friend to do any lifting and carrying. Avoid shopping or picking up heavy weights. If you're still at school, get the doctor to write a note excusing you from sports. No specific reason has to be given. Don't use tampons, go swimming, or soak in hot baths for a couple of weeks either. Although your cervix will shrink back to its normal size fairly rapidly, the increased opening to the womb makes you very vulnerable to infection after an abortion. Avoid sexual intercourse until after your next period. If you have any complications such as heavy loss of blood, bad pains, soreness or irritation you should go back to your doctor. If you can't contact anyone, go to the casualty department of your local hospital.

Abortion after 12 weeks

After 12 weeks, abortion becomes more difficult although it is still a very safe technique. Most methods involve a stay in hospital of several days. Because of the increased size of the foetus and the larger volumes of blood involved, it is not possible to suck out the contents, and using a larger tube may damage the cervix. Instead, after dilating the cervix, the doctor may insert instruments into the womb which will fragment the contents. These are then delivered from the uterus. This technique is called *Dilation and Evacuation* or *D and E*. It is carried out under general anaesthetic. D and E is very unpleasant for those performing the operation. Because of this, and the difficulties of evacuating a womb after 12 weeks, techniques have evolved which work by introducing substances into the woman's womb which cause her to have a miscarriage. One commonly used method involves first giving a local anaesthetic under the skin just above the womb and then inserting a needle into the womb to draw off some of the fluid surrounding the developing pregnancy. The fluid is then replaced either with concentrated solutions of salt and urea or a drug called prostaglandin or both. Prostaglandins are hormones which occur naturally in the body. They are responsible for contractions during labour and giving birth. Another technique involves dilating the cervix and passing a rubber tube through it into the womb. The fluids or the drug can then be introduced into the womb through the tube. Both techniques have the effect of causing the womb to begin contracting.

> 'The nurses were very nice, on the whole, but there seemed to be long stretches of time alone. It was just as well that Ann was in the other bed because we could talk to each other. I was a bit drowsy and uncomfortable while it was happening. They started me off at about 11.00 a.m. and it happened at about 8.00 p.m., though it was later for Ann. While I was lying there I couldn't help feeling angry at myself for waiting so long, and going over what I should have said to the doctor who turned me away. I still remember how it felt when it came out.'

Inducing miscarriage can be very unpleasant but is usually the safest way of performing an abortion at this stage of pregnancy. After the fluids are given to the woman she may have to wait for some hours (between 8 and 18) before the miscarriage takes place. During this time she will experience pain from the womb contracting — like labour pains. Prostaglandins cause vomiting and diarrhoea. Sedatives may be given to ease the suffering but the technique relies on the woman remaining conscious. Usually this method has to be followed up with a D and C to remove the afterbirth, which may not have come away during the miscarriage.

Hysterotomy

This is a technique now used very rarely in this country. It involves removing the contents of the womb in an operation very like a caesarean section. It is done under general anaesthetic and a woman would have to stay in hospital for a few days.

Hysterectomy

This technique would rarely be used for abortion and then only if there was no other method possible for medical reasons. It involves major surgery to remove the womb along with its contents. Most doctors would think hysterectomy an unsuitable method of abortion.

How will you feel after a late abortion?

Any abortion done after 12 weeks is likely to cause pain and cramps which may last several days as the womb shrinks back to its pre-pregnancy size. Bleeding will also go on for about a week. You will need to rest and follow the instructions given above about not swimming, soaking in a hot bath, wearing tampons or having sexual intercourse. It's usually best not to resume any of these activities until after your follow-up appointment which is normally given six weeks after the abortion.

Above all, take care of yourself. Abortion is always emotionally disturbing and you should recognise that it will take a while before you feel physically well enough to deal with any emotional consequences.

Abortion is very distressing after 12 weeks but it is an important service for those who need it. It's especially sad where the woman wanted to have a baby but found late in pregnancy that the foetus wasn't developing normally, or where a young teenager didn't recognise that she was pregnant until a few months had passed. She may have only just begun her periods and had sexual intercourse just once.

Follow-up appointment

Whether you have your abortion with one of the charities, another private clinic or through a GP other than your own, you can always go back to your own GP for a follow-up examination. The follow-up appointment charge at one of the charities is usually included in the price of the procedure, but it may be more convenient to go to your own doctor. If you decide to go to a family planning clinic for contraception after the abortion, they will do a post-abortion examination for you.

You may feel that you don't want your doctor to know, in which case returning to the doctor who helped with the abortion referral is probably the best thing to do. Don't skip this appointment. It is very important to make sure that you, your womb and your cervix have returned to good health after an abortion. If you are feeling unhappy or depressed about the abortion you could take advantage of this appointment to discuss your feelings with the doctor or ask for a referral to a counsellor. You can also use this appointment to talk about future contraception.

Is abortion dangerous?

Abortion is a very safe operation. Even the late techniques, up until about 15 weeks of pregnancy, are safer than having your tonsils out. There is always a much greater chance of serious complications or even death arising from continuing a pregnancy than from having an abortion. In England and Wales in 1984 there was only 1 death due to abortion but 52 due to complications of childbirth and pregnancy. Less than 1% of women having abortions experience any problems at the time. The likely side effects of damage to the womb, haemorrhage and infection are uncommon. The risk of encountering complications does increase with the stage of pregnancy but remains very low.

Because of the guilt associated with having an abortion many women fear that infertility will result. Research has shown these worries to be unfounded even after 2 or 3 repeat abortions. *Infertility very rarely follows uncomplicated abortion.* If it does, it is more likely to be due to other causes. Abortion by vacuum aspiration does not increase the risk of subsequent pregnancies ending in miscarriage, premature delivery or a low birthweight baby. There may be an increased risk of these complications after a late abortion but the risk is still low.

If you want to have an abortion and there are no medical reasons against it, then don't let the fear of the operation or the outcome of abortion be a factor in your decision.

Private versus NHS abortions

A recent study showed that abortion was safer in the private sector than in the NHS. These results are quite alarming but useful because they underline the need to

- reduce delays

- have good counselling

- take care of yourself after the abortion.

Also, it must be borne in mind that the results may be biased by the fact that women who are likely to suffer complications as a result of abortion are also more likely to have them done in the NHS. The abortion charities offer a very good service helping women to make their own decision about their pregnancy and then enabling them to have a safer abortion before 12 weeks, by minimising delays. Women are always told about aftercare and encouraged to be realistic about future contraception.

At worst, NHS abortion facilities offer little counselling, a lot of bureaucratic delay and no suggestions for aftercare. At best, NHS facilities are as good as anywhere.

Abortion facilities and the safety of the operation have improved considerably since the passing of the 1967 Abortion Act. Further improvements in methods of earlier detection of pregnancy, earlier abortion techniques, day care abortion services, counselling facilities, and sex education will help to reduce any remaining risks associated with abortion.

New techniques of abortion

RU 486: Successful research on a method of very early abortion currently available in France would mean that women who were less than 7 weeks pregnant could obtain abortion by taking a pill. At the moment the pill, called RU 486, which is an antiprogesterone, is still in the experimental stage in Britain. It works by bringing on a period and by stimulating the production of prostaglandins which cause contractions of the womb and expulsion of any fertilised egg. It is unlikely to be generally available for quite some time and will undoubtedly run into a debate over its legality.

Menstrual extraction: Menstrual extraction is a method of early abortion which is widely used by women in the USA to bring on

Abortion

a period. It is available on the NHS in some places and is very similar to vacuum aspiration except that it is usually only done up to about 7 weeks of pregnancy. It does not involve the powerful suction of vacuum aspiration but is sometimes called mini suction. The doctor injects a local anaesthetic into the cervix and then removes the contents of the womb via a syringe gently inserted into the womb through the cervix. Menstrual extraction is usually done in day care units or outpatient departments. A nurse to hold your hand and talk with you will provide some comfort throughout the procedure, which should take only a few minutes. Most people are ready to leave a couple of hours after the abortion. The main disadvantage of this technique, which is not at all widely available, is that it may miss the pregnancy. Some people feel that the risk of having to repeat the abortion is unacceptable and so would rather wait for a vacuum aspiration. The risk is about 1%.

Prostaglandin pessaries: This is another method of early abortion which is under investigation in some parts of Britain. It involves the insertion of a prostaglandin pessary into the vagina. This stimulates the womb to contract and dilates the cervix so that the contents of the womb are expelled. Sometimes the prostaglandins cause severe cramps or diarrhoea and vomiting. They don't always work, so some women end up having a D and C.

6. How Will You Feel After an Abortion?

Up until fairly recently it was feared that any woman who had an abortion would be seriously depressed or disturbed afterwards. Experience has shown that this is only true for a small number of women who have abortions. There are fewer women seriously distressed after an abortion than there are who suffer from postnatal depression. For many women abortion is something that affects them deeply but does not seriously interfere with their ability to manage their lives. This may be because they experience such a sense of relief at being able to control when they should or should not have a child.

For most women the overwhelming feeling after an abortion is one of relief, but the feelings of relief and control are often mixed with feelings of sadness and guilt, despite their being sure that the decision is correct: even if these negative feelings are short-lived it can be a bit confusing to feel sadness and relief at the same time.

This chapter will look at all the possible ingredients that make up your particular experience. More space is given to sad feeling, than to happy or relieved feeling. There is a lot to be gained from understanding and working through these difficult issues rather than ignoring them or pretending that they do not exist. This chapter is addressed to women but hopefully will be of value to their partners as well.

Different people react differently

Reactions to abortion will depend on your life experience, beliefs, and personality. The reactions are highly individual, yet by learning of various patterns of behaviour and reactions experienced by other women you may come to understand yourself better. You may have been most anxious before the abortion, as if you needed to do your worrying before taking action. You may have wanted to talk at great length to justify and check out the decision you were about to take, to make sure that you had missed nothing in considering what you were about to do. After the abortion you may have found that you were much calmer than you or anyone else expected.

Alternatively, at the opposite extreme, you may have found that the only way to carry out what you felt to be the right action was not to talk about it, or express any feeling, but rather to have kept tight control of all emotion, in case you were deflected from the decision you felt was right. You might have seemed very much in control beforehand; afterwards those well-controlled feelings may have escaped and need to be understood. It is almost as though such strong feelings can only be allowed out afterwards, when there is no possibility that the decision can be reversed.

If you are younger, for instance about 16 or 17 or less, you may find that you are able to put your worries about your pregnancy to one side in order to get on with your life. The pregnancy and abortion may seem unreal, because you may not have had the life experience to be affected by the emotional significance of what is happening to you. If you are older you will probably be much more aware of the conflicting feelings, especially if you have had children. Not everyone falls neatly into these categories, however. You may be the sort of person who tries to pretend that the pregnancy never existed, to run away from the experience. This may work for a time but eventually something will trigger off a reaction of some kind. Sometimes this happens when the child would have been born, or on the anniversary of the abortion, or later at the birth of a child. You may realise that you have 'left-over' feelings from an abortion when you notice other things going wrong with your life; for instance, finding that relationships with men become difficult, or your enjoyment of sex is affected. It is at this point that you may have to face up to the emotions engendered by the abortion.

Who is likely to be upset after an abortion?

It is possible to see patterns in reactions to abortion, and to say what factors are likely to make for greater or lesser distress.

You are less likely to be distressed if:

You have looked clearly at all the options facing you before deciding.

You are certain of your decision (though allowing for a small measure of doubt).

You have been able to talk over your decision with partner, friends or family and they have supported you in this.

You believed in the past that abortion was sometimes an appropriate decision.

You are more likely to be distressed if:

You have serious difficulties such as depression, anxiety, or general feelings of worry and stress, and these were present before the pregnancy.

You feel the decision has not really been yours, but forced on you by family, friends or partner.

You have been so uncertain that you have found it hard to come to a decision.

You have always believed that abortion is wrong.

You have dealt with the abortion alone and have not been able to talk openly about your decision with anyone.

You are in difficult circumstances but have been very cool and controlled before the decision.

You have had a strong negative reaction from professionals.

You have had an abortion late on in pregnancy, i.e. after twelve weeks.

You have had an abortion because you were carrying a handicapped child.

Reactions to abortion

The list below gives, very briefly, possible reactions to abortion. The aim is to give you a wide range of feelings, expressed by many women, some of which may fit you. If you have a name for the feeling you are experiencing it may help you understand more clearly what is going on inside you. Having a name for a feeling may also make it easier to explain yourself to others, and may help you feel less alone.

> Relief that you are no longer pregnant
> Relief that you do not have to be a parent before you are ready for it
> Relief that you have taken the right decision
> Strength at having taken control of your life
> Surprise and relief at the support given you by family and friends
> Closer relationship with your partner, as a result of weathering the storm together.

> Grief and/or sense of loss
> Guilt at becoming pregnant or being sexual
> Guilt at ending a potential life
> Guilt at not wanting a child
> Anger at yourself for becoming pregnant when you did not want a child
> Anger at your partner
> Anger at doctors, often because of their negative attitudes
> Revulsion against sex and sexual relationships
> Fear that you will be punished, possibly by infertility
> General sense that you are bad or unworthy.

There are two important points to note about this list. Firstly, many women feel a great sense of relief after an abortion, and this may well be the strongest feeling. Secondly, many women feel some of the harder feelings for only a relatively short time, though others find that they persist longer, and require more effort to understand and deal with. One feeling does not exclude any other and sometimes this can be most confusing, as you mentally adapt to what has happened. This is a living process during which you will experience a series of reactions.

Susan was 16 and said 'There wasn't anything else I could do. My mum would have been really hurt and let down. I didn't want a baby, it would ruin my life. Jim and I talked about it ... he would have stood by me, but I couldn't see how we would manage, so we decided on abortion, even though we didn't like the idea. Afterwards I was really relieved, because it was all over. I tried to talk to Jim but he didn't like it, he went sort of silent, I got a bit narky, and wouldn't leave him alone.'

Lynn was 22: 'It was the right man but the wrong time in our lives. We cried a lot beforehand, but it seemed to bring us closer. After I was sad but that's all. I had no doubt that it was the right decision, but it was sad; after all it was conceived in love.'

Patricia was 31, divorced with two children: 'I didn't want another child, and Paul made it clear that he wanted nothing to do with the pregnancy. But I still found it difficult. I kept on wondering what it would have looked like, whether it was a boy or a girl. I felt so ashamed — I should have known better.'

Wendy was 20: 'I couldn't do anything else, there was no question about having the baby, but I can't seem to get it out of my mind; it won't go away.'

Feelings change over time

It is hard to know when you are most likely to feel upset. Some women find that just after abortion they have one or two vivid and frightening dreams which focus on the aspect of the abortion they find hardest to deal with. For Jane it was 'In hospital, lying on a trolley, a nurse standing by me. I try to get up but can't move or speak, and she asks if I'm sure about my decision.' Jane was reliving the last possible moment when she could have changed her mind and not allowed the abortion to continue — an action she bitterly regretted.

For some women early pregnancy can be a bit like gastric flu, and they may be very relieved to feel more as they usually do. This can be followed by some distress — often quite profound —

which then eases off into a more tranquil understanding of what has happened.

Mary commented: 'After I came out of hospital I felt great, and went out shopping the next day, and out in the evening, but on the Sunday I started to bleed a bit and did not feel so good. For a couple of days I was quite depressed, I kept on thinking about what I had done, that I had ended a life, then I realised that I couldn't go on like that, after all I wouldn't have been able to give it much of a life.'

Others do not find it quite so easy to shake off these feelings and find that it takes a great deal of mental effort to forgive themselves and accept that the reasons for their decision were valid.

The question whether abortion is ending a life, or at least a potentially human life, is crucial and has to be faced, and answered to your own satisfaction. It may be you decide that by having an abortion that you did end a life, but recognise that the quality of life you would have offered would not have been adequate enough. That life may not have been welcomed and loved as it should, and that is something you would not want to happen. Perhaps certain crucial ingredients which you considered vital for a child would have been difficult to find, such as a loving father, or proper accommodation, or adequate finances. For every person who decides to end a pregnancy, there will be another who will decide to continue in apparently similar circumstances. Only you can judge whether it was the right decision for you.

Feelings of unreality

An abortion done under general anaesthetic can emphasise the sense of *unreality*, especially if there is little time between the diagnosis of the pregnancy and the admission into hospital; more so if you have not had the time to discuss your decision thoroughly with someone who is able to let you work out what you want without imposing their opinion on you. The effect of such unreality is that you can pretend to yourself that the pregnancy never happened, and therefore do not have to look at what it really meant for you. A great danger of this kind of

After an Abortion

avoidance is that you may find you become pregnant again, before you want a child.

Ann was in this position. She had become pregnant at the age of 16, within a serious relationship. When she became pregnant, she refused to tell her boyfriend and had an abortion, telling only one friend. Afterwards she ended their sexual relationship. He could not understand this and saw it as a rejection. The relationship ended and Ann became pregnant a year later after having sex with a boy at a party, when she was drunk. Looking back she realised that she had never really believed that she was pregnant, and had displaced all her anger on to her boyfriend. She avoided looking at her role, in agreeing to have a sexual relationship, because it would have meant accepting her share of responsibility for the pregnancy. She was very unsure of how to deal with her sexual feelings, and avoided sexual contact as much as possible. She had been very shocked to have a second abortion and used the crisis she was in to examine carefully the options open to her, and tried to be a bit more honest about her feelings about sex.

Grief

Grief is often experienced after abortion. It can include a sense of loss coupled with puzzlement. If you choose to have an abortion why do you feel as though you have lost something? Put another way, what right have you to grieve when you have, in effect, willed that loss? Reality is not so simple; abortion can mean a loss to you, even though you have made that choice. The loss depends on the person; it can be the loss of a child, that under different circumstances you would have wanted, or the loss of a dream of settled motherhood, with someone to love and love you, or it may be the loss of your partner if the relationship has ended. Perhaps it is a combination of these. If you feel a sadness and emptiness, it is a reality, but it will not last for ever. Denial that it exists will cause more pain than accepting the feeling. The contradiction in choosing to end a pregnancy, and yet grieving for its end, is the central dilemma of abortion. Any grief includes some guilt but after abortion you have to live with the reality that you had the choice.

Abortion

Ann commented after the second abortion: 'I was quite clear about the decision, and when you asked me about how I would feel afterwards, I remember thinking what a relief it would be, and what were you going on about it for. I was really surprised about a week after the abortion, I felt these waves of sort of thinking "you killed two babies". It was awful. I talked to my friend and she made me feel a bit better when she said that it would have been really awful for those children, if I had had to bring them up in my circumstances and feeling the way I did.'

Guilt

Guilt can make you feel generally bad and worthless, rather than focusing as it did with Ann on the actual abortion. It can make you feel that you deserve punishment. Many women have said that they feared that they would not be able to have children when they wanted to, because of the abortion. Another more dangerous effect is when you behave in ways which invite disaster, thereby proving to yourself that you are unworthy.

Alice found it difficult to settle down after her abortion and found herself in silly situations which did her no good; she could not bring herself to study so she started to fall badly behind in her work. Fortunately she spoke to her GP who realised that she was quite upset and depressed, and that this related directly to the abortion. Alice talked about her feelings about the abortion, and as she did so began to see that she felt she should be punished for her abortion and felt she did not deserve to succeed in anything. Alice thought carefully about what had happened and how she felt, and eventually realised that the decision to have an abortion was pointless if she became so depressed that she could not do those very things that she had felt were so important.

Sometimes you can drift into unsuitable relationships, which, instead of making you feel valued and loved, do the opposite. If you think carefully you may be able to see a direct link between these damaging relationships and your abortion. You may find that you have a generalised feeling of *depression*, rather than experiencing some of the individual feelings described earlier.

Feelings of worthlessness are sometimes translated into the sexual arena. *Sarah* was a young student who almost against her conscious wishes had sex with a number of different men at parties. It was not until her friend's boyfriend said 'What on earth are you doing to yourself,' that she began to realise that something was quite wrong. Discussions showed that she was very ashamed of having had an abortion; and feeling bad about herself, saw no point in refusing to have sex with someone she did not care about, especially as she saw herself as a worthless creature. Unfortunately, although she enjoyed a brief sensation of being wanted, she usually felt even worse about herself afterwards.

Effects on your relationship

Abortion can change the relationships that you are already in. It can change what was a good relationship into a more uncertain and difficult relationship. It can also show whether your relationship is strong enough to adapt to change, or difficulty, and can deal with a crisis.

Susan met her boyfriend in the summer between school and university; she had never had a sexual relationship before and was very romantic. The relationship was exciting and she felt that contraception would spoil its spontaneity. When she discovered that she was pregnant her boyfriend could not cope, and the relationship ended. Susan always felt that something best described as her innocence died in the process.

Lynn was also deeply and romantically in love with her boyfriend, though older than Susan. Her pregnancy was upsetting to both of them but they realised that there was no way in which they could have the child as they had no housing or money and both had ambitious plans for the future. After the abortion they felt that they had shared the decision and the sadness, and that they felt much closer than before. They are now married.

Sometimes, unconsciously, a woman tests a relationship by becoming pregnant; if her partner fails the test, she loses baby and relationship. *Elspeth* realised afterwards what had happened: 'Jimmy was never sure whether he would stay with me or try to make a go of his marriage. I used to resent this and specially all the talk about his children. Looking back I used to feel quite lonely and I half wondered what he would do if I became pregnant. I did, and he just could not cope, and that was the end of it all. In a way I'm glad I realised before it was too late. It had all been going on far too long and was not doing me much good.'

Anger

Anger is a common feeling. You blame others for what has happened — the man you were or are involved with, the circumstances which left you vulnerable, or the doctors whom you saw. You may have good reason to feel let down, but you may be avoiding the difficult task of looking at how you found yourself in this situation. This is as unhelpful as shouldering all the blame for an unwanted pregnancy. Angry reactions can be complicated. When *Wendy* found she was pregnant, she ended the relationship with Peter and would not let him share the decision about the pregnancy. It was not clear whether she was punishing herself or Peter or, finding that she could trust no one, taking all the responsibility herself.

Catherine on the other hand was quite clear how she felt: 'I told him I was pregnant and he just looked at me and said "Well, how do I know its mine?" I just could not believe it.' This happens depressingly often. Catherine was justifiably angry but later recognised that she herself had not taken any responsibility for contraception.

Numbness

It may be easier in the short term to cope with the inherent contradiction of abortion by a kind of distancing or *numbness* which does not interfere with everyday life but avoids dealing with occasionally painful feelings. This can be useful in allowing time to adapt to your loss. You may not fully realise how you are feeling until something happens to make you aware that you are not feeling the way you normally do and it is time to look at what is really going on inside.

Sexual difficulties

When you are feeling numb, it can be hard to relate closely to anyone, particularly sexually. If sex has led to pregnancy and abortion, then it can take some time before sex can seem safe or attractive. If you feel that your partner was to blame, or that he was not as supportive as he might have been, then it can be a way of punishing him to withdraw from sex. Some people have long-term sexual problems after abortion but usually there were some difficulties beforehand.

Difficulties with sex can often stem from your opinions about the place of sex in your life. For instance, if you believe strongly that it is wrong to have premarital sex, then you might feel uneasy if you enter into a sexual relationship, especially if you do so under pressure. If you then become pregnant, and do not wish to continue with it, you might then be very uneasy about sex and find it hard to enjoy it or become aroused. Probably the most likely difficulty is a lack of interest/or pleasure in sex, and with it some pain on intercourse, possibly due to lack of arousal. A particularly unpleasant internal examination could make you afraid of a man penetrating you, and you therefore contract the muscles around the vagina in order to protect yourself. This causes pain when sex is attempted. This can be helped given time and trust in your partner.

There are now more places able to give help with specific sexual problems, as well as with general feelings of anxiety about sex. Your GP, local family planning clinic, or hospital should have information, as well as agencies such as your local Marriage Guidance Counselling Service, Brook Advisory Centres and Citizens Advice Bureaux.

Feelings after rape or incest

If you are pregnant as a result of rape or incest, then you may experience some of the feelings described earlier, but the pregnancy is probably a relatively small part of a much greater problem. If you are feeling very ashamed and humiliated rather than angry, you may find it difficult to admit to others what has happened. If you can bring yourself to talk to someone about it, that alone will bring tremendous relief. If you are afraid of rejection or judgement, contact an agency such as Rape Crisis Centre who will help with feelings about incest as well, and they will advise you. The agencies mentioned above, as well as your GP, should also be able to help you appropriately.

Feelings after a late abortion

The discomfort of labour, and its ending with nothing to show, brings the reality of abortion home very forcibly. You may find that you dwell on the experience itself, and find it quite upsetting.

Apart from this you are likely to feel the same range of feelings as those who have abortion done under anaesthetic, possibly with more emphasis on the negative aspects, especially if you were advised to have the abortion for medical reasons.

Positive feelings

As often happens, there is more to say about the sad and difficult feelings than about the happier ones. *Mary* epitomised the positive feelings that abortion can bring. She was twenty and had already lost both parents, and her marriage had ended after two years. She had a son of three from that marriage, there had been a miscarriage which had also upset her, as at that stage she wanted another child. After the marriage ended she decided to start a small business and about three months before becoming pregnant had met a man she cared a good deal for. She was using a cap as her method of contraception because she had not liked the pill, but became pregnant soon after they started a sexual relationship. She decided on abortion, as she felt that it was too soon for them to become parents and she was not yet ready to cope with another child. She feared that she might feel as she had done after the miscarriage but after it was all over she said 'I feel fine, no regrets, but a feeling that for once I was in control of my life, not the other way round.'

Methods of coping

Honesty and forgiveness are the central themes of coping with abortion. There is little point pretending to feel sad or relieved when it is not true; a pretence of this kind makes it harder to cope, not easier. Sometimes it is not very easy to know what one feels and it may take time and help to unravel one's feelings. This *understanding* of your feelings is a step towards coming to terms with your abortion. The next stage is to *forgive* yourself so that you can move on to the next stage in your life.

This process can be helped by *talking* to others, such as friends, family or your partner; or alternatively to people such as doctors, social workers or counsellors. Those close to you can offer affection and support, and are there when you need them. It is good if they can allow you to be yourself with them, but sometimes they are less able to stand back and allow you to work things out for yourself, partly because they do not always realise how important this is. When you are angry they are more likely to stand by you than to challenge whether that anger is, for instance, appropriate. A friend is more likely to tell you what you want to hear than a counsellor. Usually people need both kinds of care.

Talking, and for some people *writing*, is a way of separating the different feelings and naming them. Give yourself time and particularly a sense of peace and calm, in a pleasant place. If alone, write down answers to certain simple questions, or try to discuss these questions with someone. It is important to write or speak because having to explain and make sense to others is also a way of making sense to yourself. Do not worry if there are contradictions because feelings are rarely simple and in unravelling the contradictions you will begin to understand more clearly. The tolerance of the other person who is listening to your convoluted thinking, or the blankness of that piece of paper, will give you the courage to be honest.

Questions that help are open-ended, they do not invite the answer yes or no. What was the worst thing about the pregnancy/abortion? How did you feel when you discovered you were pregnant, you spoke to the doctor, you told your partner,

Abortion

you saw the gynaecologist, you went into hospital, you left hospital and what happened at each stage? Describing what happened and how you felt at each stage will be very helpful in understanding your feelings, and questions such as what do you mean by, for instance guilt, or upset, or relief, can be helpful in clarifying what was going on for you in particular.

You might find it useful to look at the list given earlier in the chapter about possible reactions to abortion to see if they fit how you feel; even if there is no resemblance, thinking about the difference between you and what is described might be helpful.

If you are in a close relationship with a man you might feel that you ought to be able to share all that you feel with him. Sometimes this is possible, but if both of you are upset by the abortion you might find that your speaking about the abortion upsets the other (or vice versa) and makes it difficult to handle things between you. This can be particularly hard for those couples who have told no one else about the abortion. This is why there is sometimes an increase in tension between couples afterwards; the feelings need to be spread more widely and both partners need the opportunity to talk about their feelings without the fear of hurting the other, and therefore with someone else.

Understanding what you feel, along with *acceptance* that it has happened, then *forgiving* yourself are all helpful in coping with abortion. Forgiveness does not mean denying pain or mistakes made but it is a kind of peace-making which allows you to move forward to the next stage in your life. You may find that it is not complete and that you will in the future still go over what happened but it is part of learning to live with yourself.

Sometimes in this process there is the need to mark or commemorate what happened. Japanese women mark the loss of a potential child by lighting a candle at a shrine. Some women might choose to do something similar in church or at home. Others feel that they want to mark what has happened by giving time, perhaps to a charity that helps children, or by giving money to such an organisation.

Looking back

When you are looking back at your decision to seek an abortion it is helpful to remember why you felt it was best; if it is written down it will be there to read later on and to remind yourself. Isolation makes you more anxious; in deciding that you cannot tell your story, you are living out your belief that it is too bad to tell. No story is too bad to tell, and in believing that, you are forgetting that others make mistakes and that we all learn from our mistakes.

It is important that the sadness and loss and guilt be linked with the strong and positive, and be turned in some way into something positive. It would be sad if the abortion were a marker on a downward spiral rather than a step towards a more content self. This is why forgiveness is so important. Even if it is a long time since you have had your abortion, it is never too late to look at how you feel and how it has affected your life.

Talking with others

It is sometimes helpful to talk to other people who have had an abortion. Some organisations such as the Women's Therapy Centre in London run groups of this kind. The idea is to share experiences and to help come to terms with the feelings involved.

If you are interested in this, contact your local family planning clinic or Brook Advisory Centre. If they do not know of any such groups, they might be willing to help you organise a group.

For addresses see p. 81.

7. Some Final Words

Future contraception

Your body may take as little as 10 days to again begin releasing ova (eggs) after an abortion, so you must be ready to use contraception as soon as you resume sexual intercourse.

You may be thinking that you don't need contraception because you will not be having sex again, for a while anyway. But are you being realistic? Wouldn't it be better to be prepared?

The evidence shows that women who don't settle on a method of contraception after an abortion are quite likely to end up with another unwanted pregnancy.

There are three methods of contraception you may be tempted to ask for — or feel pressurised into accepting — at the time of the abortion. Sterilisation, the injectable contraceptive, and the IUD. Because sterilisation is irreversible it would be unwise to accept this at the time of the abortion. The decision to be sterilised should be separated from abortion. You are far more likely to feel regret if you agree to sterilisation at the same time as abortion than if you decide to have it done later. The risk of complications increases when sterilisation and abortion are done together.

The injectable contraceptive lasts for three months, and can cause problems with your periods, so you may want time to decide whether this method would be suitable for you. As for the IUD, since this can easily be removed, the decision to have it put in at the time of the abortion is less serious. Nevertheless don't feel pressurised into having an IUD either. It is your right to say No.

Think carefully about which method of contraception would suit you best.

> Weigh up the risks involved. For example, the pill is the safest method, but does have side effects. Is it better to risk the side effects and have absolute security or the other way round?

Some Final Words

Decide which method suits your lifestyle. For example, some women do not lead the sort of lives where it is likely that they will remember to take the pill regularly, but would be able to use sheaths or the diaphragm, or may prefer an IUD.

Discuss with your partner which one of you is going to take responsibility for contraception.

Write to the Family Planning Association, 27/35 Mortimer Street, London W1N 7RJ for their leaflets on methods of birth control, or drop into your family doctor or family planning clinic for them.

You may find it useful to go to see a doctor with your partner. Many women find that resolving the problem of an unwanted pregnancy with their partner improves the intimacy of their relationship, and issues like pregnancy and contraception are raised for the first time.

Try to make sure it is the last time you have to face an abortion decision.

Remember

Some of the delays you will encounter when seeking abortion are out of your control. Some are not. Don't waste time wondering if you are pregnant, but seek help immediately. Chase up your doctor if appointments by post have not come through and don't let anyone make you wait. Some physicians may suggest you go away and think things over. If you have made up your mind, don't agree to this. If you have not and you are feeling uncertain about what to do, it will probably be worth setting the process in motion anyway. You can always change your mind at the last minute. If you do change your mind, don't be afraid to say so.

Talk to others about your predicament, but take your own decision and don't let others pressure you.

Find out as much as you can about what to expect and ask as many questions as you want.

Make sure you have support from someone close to you.

Be sure to plan for the future.

Useful Addresses

General information

British Association for Counselling, 1a Little Church Street, Rugby, Warwickshire. Tel. 0788 7328.
Phone or write for a list of counselling and advisory centres in your area offering help with problems concerning sex and personal relationships.

National Association of Young People's Counselling and Advisory Services (NAYPCAS), 17-23 Albion Street, Leicester LE1 6GD. Tel. 0533 554775.
Phone or write for a list of local counselling and information services for young people.

The Well Woman Centre, 60 Eccles Street, Dublin 1 (tel: Dublin 728051/381365) or 63 Lower Leeson Street, Dublin 2 (tel: Dublin 789366/789504).
The Well Woman Centre provides general health screening, diagnosis of sexually transmitted diseases, diagnosis of pregnancy, help with contraception, pregnancy counselling and counselling in sexual and emotional problems.

Child Poverty Action Group (CPAG), 1 Macklin Street, London WC2. Tel. 01-242 9149.
Acts as an information research and monitoring body of welfare policies. Publishes welfare rights guides, journals, and bulletins on the social security system.

Shelter Housing Aid Centres, National Housing Aid Trust, 157 Waterloo Road, London SE1 8UU. Tel. 01-633 9377.
Shelter is the national campaign for the homeless. They have a network of housing aid centres to help with housing problems. Shelter Scotland, tel: 031-226 6347; Shelter Wales, tel: 0792 469400.

Useful Addresses

Pregnancy testing, counselling and referral for abortion
(see chapters 2 and 4)

Your GP
Contact your local post office, library, Citizens Advice Bureau, Community Health Council or Family Practitioner Committee for addresses of family doctors in your area.

Brook Advisory Centres
19 centres in 6 cities in England and Scotland. Contact their Central Office for details 153a East Street, London SE17 2SD. Tel. 01-708 1234. Also provide contraceptive advice and supplies, especially for young people under 25.

Family planning clinics
Look in telephone directory for your local clinic or find out the address and telephone number from the Family Planning Association Clinic Enquiry Service at 27-35 Mortimer Street, London W1N 7RJ. Tel. 01-636 7866.

Abortion charities
British Pregnancy Advisory Service, Austy Manor, Wootton Wawen, Solihull, West Midlands B95 6BX. Tel. Henley in Arden 05642 3225. Branches in Basingstoke, Birmingham, Bournemouth, Bradford, Brighton, Cardiff, Chester, Coventry, Doncaster, Glasgow, Hull, Leamington Spa, Leeds, Liverpool, London, Luton, Manchester, Milton Keynes, Sheffield and Swindon.

Telephone the head office for details of your local centre or look in the telephone directory or yellow pages under *Family Planning*.

Pregnancy Advisory Service, 11-13 Charlotte Street, London W1P 1HD. Tel. 01-637 8962.

Marie Stopes, Marie Stopes House, 108 Whitfield Street, London W1. Tel. 01-388 0662.

The abortion charities also provide aftercare and information on contraception.

Abortion

Northern Ireland
Ulster Pregnancy Advisory Association, 719a Lisburn Road, Belfast BT9 7GU. Tel. 0232 667345.
Offer pregnancy counselling, arrange appointments with clinics in England and provide aftercare.

Organisations offering advice, counselling and support
(see Chapter 3)

British Agencies for Adoption and Fostering 11 Southwark Street, London SE1 1RQ. Tel. 01-407 8800.
Provide advice on adoption and fostering. Produce free leaflets.

One-Parent Families 255 Kentish Town Road, London NW5. Tel. 01-267 1361.
Offer free confidential advice to single parents and single pregnant women. Campaign to improve the law and services for one-parent families. Produce free leaflets.

Scottish Council for Single Parents 13 Gayfield Square, Edinburgh EH1 3NX. Tel. 031-556 3899; 39 Hope Street, Glasgow G2 6AE. Tel. 041-248 3488.
Advice and information for single parents.

Gingerbread 35 Wellington Street, London WC2. Tel. 01-240 0953/4.
Self-help association for single parents; over 400 local groups.

Release 347a Upper Street, London N1. Tel. 01-837 5606.
24-hour emergency telephone advice line.

Life Head Office, 7 Parade, Leamington Spa, Warwickshire CV32 4DG. Tel. 0926 21587; Scottish Office, 4th Floor, 38 Bath Street, Glasgow G2. Tel. 041-332 9656.
An organisation opposed to abortion. Has offices all over the country offering pregnancy testing, counselling and temporary accommodation for homeless and unsupported pregnant women and mothers. Phone or write to above for details of your nearest office or look in the telephone directory or local paper.

Rape Crisis Centres P.O. Box 69, London WC1X 9NJ. Tel. (office hours) 01-278 3965; emergency service 01-837 1600.
There are many local centres. Office details and emergency telephone numbers are noted in telephone directories, available from Citizens Advice Bureaux or advertised in public places.
Rape Crisis offer counselling, medical and legal advice and will arrange and accompany women on appointments to doctors, police and courts.

Choice P.O. Box 20, Oxford. Tel. Oxford 242333.
A telephone counselling service to help women come to a decision as to whether they want an abortion *and* to give information and support to those who choose abortion.

Safta (support after termination for foetal abnormality) 22 Upper Woburn Place, London WC1H 0EP. Post abortion counselling. An organisation hoping to develop a nationwide network of support for women suffering termination of pregnancy after foetal abnormality. Send s.a.e. for details.

Support groups for women coming to Britain for abortion

Abortion Support for Spanish Women
Support and advice for women coming from Spain to London for abortion.
c/o Womens Health Information Centre. Tel. 01-251 6580 (01-251 6332).

Irish Women's Abortion Support Group
Support and advice for women coming to London from Ireland for abortion.
c/o Women's Reproductive Rights Campaign. Tel. 01-251 6332

Contraception

Family Planning Information Service (FPIS).
Provides information, including leaflets, posters and publications — to ensure that people know about and use the free National Health Family Planning facilities. Stocks of FPIS literature are held locally by FPA Regional Administrators.

London Office FPA   27-35 Mortimer Street, London W1N 7RJ. Tel. 01-636 7866.

Scottish Office FPA   4 Clifton Street, Glasgow G3 7LA. Tel. 041-333 0496.

Northern Ireland FPA   47 Botanic Avenue, Belfast BT7 1JL. Tel. 0232 225488.

Wales FPA   6 Windsor Place, Cardiff. Tel. 0222 387471.

For contraceptive advice and supplies contact your GP; your local family planning clinic or a Brook advisory centre (see above for details).

Organisations campaigning to improve abortion law and for service provision

Abortion Law Reform Association, 88a Islington High Street, London N1 Tel. 01-359 5200. Produce magazine 'Breaking Chains' six times a year.

Co-ord (Co-ordinating Committee in Defence of the 1967 Abortion Act), 27-35 Mortimer Street, London W1. Tel. 01-580 9360.

National Abortion Campaign, 70 Great Queen Street, London WC2B 5AX.

Northern Ireland Abortion Law Reform Association, P.O. Box 151, Belfast BT9 6FT.

Northern Ireland Abortion Campaign, c/o The Women's Centre, 18 Lower Donegal Street, Belfast 1.

Scottish Abortion Campaign, c/o Glasgow Women's Centre, 48 Miller Street, Glasgow. Tel. 041-423 5197 or 041-334 7556.

Womens Reproductive Rights Campaign, 52 Featherstone Street, London EC1. Tel. 01-6580/6589.

Further Reading

Personal experiences and practical advice

Mixed Feelings by Brent Against Corrie pamphlet group
Women's Reproductive Right Information Centre, 1983. Ten women talk about their experience of pregnancy and abortion.

Mixed Feelings by Angela Neustatter and Gina Newson.
Pluto Press, 1986.
The human experience of abortion — a collection of detailed interviews with women and men.

Abortion — Not an easy choice by Kathleen McDonnell.
Women's Press of Canada, 1984.
A feminist re-examines feelings about and motives for seeking abortion.

Our bodies, Ourselves by Angela Phillips and Jill Rakusen.
Penguin, 1986.
A health book for women which includes a section on techniques of abortion, the need for aftercare and a discussion on the emotions involved.

Abortion

The Ambivalence of Abortion by Lynda Bird Francke.
Penguin, 1980.
A compassionate, personal account of the feelings surrounding the decision to terminate a pregnancy.

The Single Woman's Guide to Pregnancy and Parenthood by Patricia Ashdown Sharp.
Penguin, 1975.
Covers a variety of topics including pregnancy, abortion, adoption, single parenthood, contraception.

Political and ethical issues

Causing Death and Saving Lives by Jonathan Glover.
Pelican, 1977.
An examination of the morality and philosophy of abortion.

Abortion: The Personal Dilemma by R.F.R. Gardner.
The Paternoster Press, 1977.
A study of the medical, social and spiritual issues of abortion, written by a Christian gynaecologist.

Abortion and the Politics of Motherhood by Kristin Luker.
University of California Press, 1984.
A sensitive study of activists in the pro choice and anti abortion pressure groups.

Abortion Politics by D. Marsh and J. Chambers.
Birth Control Trust, 1980.
An academic survey of parliamentary decision-making which traces the progress of the Corrie Abortion Amendment bill.

Abortion — The Irish Question by Andrew Rynne.
Ward River Press, Dublin, 1983.
A detailed and sensitive account of public and parliamentary attitudes to abortion in Eire and Northern Ireland.

Abortion in Demand by Victoria Greenwood and J. Young.
Pluto Press, 1976.
An emotional discussion of the history and impact of abortion law in Britain.

Historical and sociological

Abortion Law Reformed by Madeleine Simms and Keith Hindell. Peter Owen, 1971.
A historical account of public and parliamentary process leading to the reform of law on abortion in Britain.

Abortion by Malcolm Potts, Peter Diggory and John Peel. Cambridge University Press, 1977.
Worldwide data on historical, sociological, clinical and demographic aspects of abortion.

Counselling in Unwanted Pregnancy by Juliet Cheetham. Routlege and Kegan Paul, 1977.
An academic analysis of the social and psychological background to unwanted pregnancy. A training guide to ways of offering support.

Abortion Freedom — A worldwide movement by Colin Francome Allen and Unwin, 1984.
Discusses the worldwide controversies surrounding the abortion issue. Aimed at students of politics and law but of interest to the general reader.

Why Discuss Abortion? A work pack for use with young people providing information on the history of abortion, abortion facilities and methods of abortion. The exercises and case studies included are designed to trigger discussion for group participation. Written and published by ALRA, 88a Islington High Street, London N1 8EG.

Abortion

Contraception

Free leaflets on family planning, sex education and women's health care are produced by the Family Planning Information Service. Ask for an order form from 27/35 Mortimer Street, London W1N 7RJ or ask at your family planning clinic or health centre.

An Introduction to Family Planning by Toni Belfield and Helen Martins.
FPA, 1984.
An excellent illustrated booklet for 60p. Available from FPA.

Choices in Contraception by Zandra Pauncefort.
Pan, 1984.
Provides a clear description of all available methods of contraception and discusses which method is best for you, what the side effects are and how it will affect your relationship.

Contraception — The Facts by Peter Bromwich and Tony Parsons.
Oxford Medical Publications, 1984.
A very concise, straightforward account of all contraceptive methods available with instructions for use and the advantages and disadvantages of each.
This book contains information for special group, the young, the over 35s, diabetics, epileptics, the disabled and people from racial or religious groups. Advice is also given for people considering abortion. Finally, there is a clear description of current research in contraception and methods likely to be available in future.